End Time Prophecy: A Complete Biblical Study

"The testimony of Jesus is the spirit of prophecy." – **Revelation 19:10**

1. Introduction: Why Study End Time Prophecy?

End time prophecy is not about fear—it's about **faith**. The Bible doesn't hide the future; it reveals it to prepare God's people.
"Surely the Lord GOD will do nothing, but He revealeth His secret unto His servants the prophets." – *Amos 3:7*

From Genesis to Revelation, the Bible unfolds a divine timeline. God's people are not left in darkness about what is to come. **"But ye, brethren, are not in darkness, that that day should overtake you as a thief."** – *1 Thessalonians 5:4*

2. The Purpose of Prophecy

The goal of prophecy is not to satisfy curiosity, but to:
Point us to **Jesus Christ**
Warn the world of judgment
Encourage believers to live holy lives
Build endurance and hope
"He that hath this hope in him purifieth himself, even as He is pure." – *1 John 3:3*

3. Key Themes in End Time Prophecy

A. The Second Coming of Christ
The most repeated prophecy in the New Testament is the **return of Jesus**.
"And if I go and prepare a place for you, I will come again..." – *John 14:3* **"Behold, He cometh with clouds; and every eye shall see Him."** – *Revelation 1:7*

B. The Rise of a Global Leader (Antichrist)
The Bible speaks of a final world ruler known as the "man of sin" or the Antichrist.
"Let no man deceive you... that man of sin be revealed... who

opposeth and exalteth himself above all that is called God." – *2 Thessalonians 2:3–4*

C. The Great Tribulation

A time of global chaos, persecution, and divine judgment.

"For then shall be great tribulation, such as was not since the beginning of the world..." – *Matthew 24:21*

D. The Rapture and Resurrection of the Saints

The "catching away" of believers, dead and alive.

"The dead in Christ shall rise first... we which are alive... shall be caught up together with them in the clouds." – *1 Thessalonians 4:16–17*

E. The Millennial Reign of Christ

Jesus will reign on earth for 1,000 years with His saints.

"They lived and reigned with Christ a thousand years." – *Revelation 20:4*

F. The Final Judgment

God will judge all mankind at the Great White Throne.

"And whosoever was not found written in the book of life was cast into the lake of fire." – *Revelation 20:15*

4. Jesus' Prophetic Outline (Matthew 24)

The clearest end time prophecy from Jesus Himself is found in **Matthew 24:**

False Christs and false prophets (v. 5, 11)
Wars and rumors of wars (v. 6)
Famines, pestilences, and earthquakes (v. 7)
Persecution of believers (v. 9)
Gospel preached to all nations (v. 14)
The abomination of desolation (v. 15)
Great tribulation (v. 21)
Cosmic signs and shaking (v. 29)
The return of Christ (v. 30)
Gathering of the elect (v. 31)
"When ye shall see all these things, know that it is near, even at the doors." – *Matthew 24:33*

5. Daniel's Prophecies and the 70 Weeks

Daniel's visions lay the foundation for all end time prophecy.

"Seventy weeks are determined upon thy people…" – *Daniel 9:24*

This prophecy describes:

69 weeks (483 years) to the Messiah's arrival

The Messiah being "cut off" (crucified)

A pause (church age)

The 70th week (7 years of tribulation)

"And he shall confirm the covenant with many for one week…" – *Daniel 9:27*

This final 7-year period is the **tribulation**, split into two halves (see Revelation 11 and 13).

6. The Rise of the Antichrist

A powerful global leader will rise, backed by Satan:

"The dragon gave him his power, and his seat, and great authority." – *Revelation 13:2*

He will:

Make a covenant with Israel (Daniel 9:27)

Break it after 3.5 years (Daniel 9:27)

Demand worship (2 Thessalonians 2:4)

Control buying and selling via the "mark of the beast" (Revelation 13:17)

7. The Mark of the Beast

Revelation 13 details a global system of control:

"And he causeth all... to receive a mark... that no man might buy or sell, save he that had the mark." - *Revelation 13:16–17*

The number of the beast is **666**. Refusing the mark will result in persecution and death—but accepting it results in eternal judgment.

"If any man worship the beast... he shall be tormented... forever." *– Revelation 14:9–11*

8. The Rapture: A Sudden Catching Away

Paul taught about the rapture in **1 Thessalonians 4**:

"Then we which are alive and remain shall be caught up... to meet the Lord in the air." – *1 Thessalonians 4:17*

This event is:

Sudden (1 Corinthians 15:52)

Before God's wrath (1 Thessalonians 5:9)

A hope for believers (Titus 2:13)

9. The Great Tribulation

Jesus described a time of **unparalleled distress**:

"Such as was not since the beginning of the world." –
Matthew 24:21
During this time:
21 judgments fall (seals, trumpets, bowls) – Revelation 6–16
One-third of the world dies (Revelation 9:18)
Earthquakes, plagues, and famine escalate
Persecution of saints and Jews intensifies
This period ends with **Christ's visible return**.

10. The Second Coming of Christ

Jesus returns **in glory**, not as a lamb, but as a **King** and **Judge**.

"Behold, the Lord cometh with ten thousands of His saints." – *Jude 1:14*
"Every eye shall see Him." – *Revelation 1:7*
He defeats the Antichrist (Revelation 19), binds Satan (Revelation 20:1–3), and establishes His kingdom.

11. The Millennial Reign of Christ

Christ will rule on earth for **1,000 years**:
"They shall be priests of God... and shall reign with Him a thousand years." – *Revelation 20:6*
This reign fulfills promises to:
Israel (land and kingdom restored)
The church (reigning with Christ – 2 Timothy 2:12)

Creation (restored peace – Isaiah 11:6–9)

12. The Final Rebellion and Judgment

After 1,000 years, Satan is released and deceives the nations one last time (Revelation 20:7–10). God destroys the rebellion, and the **Great White Throne Judgment** follows.

"And I saw a great white throne, and Him that sat on it..." – *Revelation 20:11*

Every unbeliever is judged by their works. Those not in the Book of Life are cast into the **lake of fire** (v. 15).

13. New Heaven and New Earth

After final judgment, God creates a new heaven and earth:

"And I saw a new heaven and a new earth... for the first heaven and the first earth were passed away." – *Revelation 21:1*

He dwells with His people forever:

"God shall wipe away all tears... there shall be no more death, neither sorrow..." – *Revelation 21:4*

The New Jerusalem descends, a glorious eternal home for the redeemed (Revelation 21–22).

14. What Should We Do Now?

A. Watch and Be Ready

"Watch therefore: for ye know not what hour your Lord doth come." – *Matthew 24:42*

B. Live Holy and Godly Lives

"Seeing... all these things shall be dissolved, what manner of persons ought ye to be in all holy conversation and godliness." – *2 Peter 3:11*

C. Preach the Gospel

"And this gospel of the kingdom shall be preached... and then shall the end come." – *Matthew 24:14*

D. Encourage One Another

"Wherefore comfort one another with these words." – *1 Thessalonians 4:18*

15. Conclusion: Jesus Is Coming Soon

Prophecy is not a puzzle—it's a promise.

"Surely I come quickly." Amen. Even so, come, Lord Jesus." – *Revelation 22:20*

Jesus is coming soon—not just as a Savior, but as King and Judge. End time prophecy calls us to repentance, hope, and readiness.

✓ Summary Table: Timeline of End Time Events
Event
Scripture
Rapture of the Church
1 Thess. 4:16–17
Rise of Antichrist

2 Thess. 2:3–4
7-Year Tribulation
Daniel 9:27, Rev. 6–16
Second Coming of Christ
Rev. 19:11–16
Millennial Reign
Rev. 20:1–6
Final Judgment
Rev. 20:11–15
New Heaven and Earth
Rev. 21:1–4

16. The Role of Israel in End Time Prophecy

Understanding end time prophecy requires understanding **God's**

covenant with Israel. God is not finished with the Jewish people. **"And so all Israel shall be saved: as it is written..."** – *Romans 11:26*

A. The Regathering of Israel

Prophecy foretold that Israel would be scattered and then regathered to her land:

"I will take you from among the heathen, and gather you out of all countries." – *Ezekiel 36:24*

In 1948, Israel became a nation again—after nearly 2,000 years—fulfilling this prophecy.

B. Jerusalem: The Prophetic Clock

Jerusalem is at the center of end time events:

"I will make Jerusalem a burdensome stone for all people..." – *Zechariah 12:3*

"Jerusalem shall be trodden down... until the times of the Gentiles be fulfilled." – *Luke 21:24*

C. The Covenant with the Antichrist

The Antichrist will make a 7-year covenant with Israel (Daniel 9:27), which he will break midway through. This act will trigger the **Great Tribulation**, especially directed at Israel.

"When ye therefore shall see the abomination of desolation... flee into the mountains." – *Matthew 24:15–16*

17. The Two Witnesses (Revelation 11)

During the tribulation, God will raise up two prophetic witnesses: **"And I will give power unto My two witnesses, and they shall prophesy... clothed in sackcloth."** – *Revelation 11:3*

They will perform miracles

Preach boldly for 1,260 days

Be killed by the beast

Be resurrected and caught up to heaven

Their ministry will be a **final call to repentance** during extreme darkness.

18. The 144,000 (Revelation 7 and 14)

God will seal 144,000 Jewish believers to be protected and serve as witnesses:

"A hundred and forty and four thousand of all the tribes of the children of Israel." – *Revelation 7:4*

These are not Jehovah's Witnesses or symbolic numbers—they are literal Jewish believers, protected by God, evangelizing during the Tribulation.

19. The Global Revival and Martyrdom

Despite judgment, the Tribulation will include a **great harvest of souls**:

"A great multitude... of all nations... stood before the throne." – *Revelation 7:9*

They came "out of great tribulation" (v. 14), meaning many will turn to Christ—even at the cost of their lives.

"They loved not their lives unto the death." – *Revelation 12:11*

20. Babylon the Great: Religious and Political Systems

Revelation 17 and 18 describe **Mystery Babylon**, a symbol of end time apostasy and corruption.

Chapter 17: Spiritual/religious Babylon – false religion and persecution

Chapter 18: Economic/political Babylon – the global system of greed and trade

"Babylon the great is fallen, is fallen..." – *Revelation 18:2*

God will destroy this system **suddenly**, just before Christ's return.

21. The Marriage Supper of the Lamb

Before returning with Christ, the Church will be united with Him in heaven:

"Blessed are they which are called unto the marriage supper of the Lamb." – *Revelation 19:9*

This glorious celebration is for the **bride of Christ**—those who were faithful, pure, and ready.

"His wife hath made herself ready." – *Revelation 19:7*

22. The Return of Christ in Glory

Christ will return visibly, powerfully, and in righteousness:

"And I saw heaven opened, and behold a white horse..." – *Revelation 19:11*
"Out of His mouth goeth a sharp sword... and He treadeth the winepress of the fierceness of the wrath of Almighty God." – *Revelation 19:15*
He defeats the Antichrist, casts the beast and false prophet into the lake of fire (Revelation 19:20), and begins His **millennial reign**.

23. Satan Bound and Released

After Christ's return:
"An angel... laid hold on the dragon... and bound him a thousand years." – *Revelation 20:1–2*

Satan is bound during the millennium. Afterward, he is released for a short time, gathers a final rebellion (Gog and Magog), and is **finally defeated** forever. **"And the devil... was cast into the lake of fire... and shall be tormented day and night forever."** – *Revelation 20:10*

24. The Final Judgment (Great White Throne)

Every unbeliever throughout history will stand before God: **"And I saw the dead, small and great, stand before God... and the books were opened."** – *Revelation 20:12*

Those not found in the Book of Life will be judged by their works—none of which can save. **"This is the second death."** – *Revelation 20:14*

25. The New Heaven and Earth (Revelation 21–22)

Sin and sorrow are forever gone. God makes all things new: **"And I saw a new heaven and a new earth."** – *Revelation 21:1*

In this eternal state:

God dwells with man (Revelation 21:3)

No more death, pain, or crying (Revelation 21:4)

The New Jerusalem is our eternal home (Revelation 21:10–27)

The river of life and tree of life are restored (Revelation 22:1–2)

26. The Spirit and the Bride Say "Come"

God's final words are not judgment, but invitation:

"And the Spirit and the bride say, Come. And let him that heareth say, Come." – *Revelation 22:17*

God longs to save. The door is still open.

"Whosoever will, let him take the water of life freely."

27. Final Warnings and Encouragements

A. Don't Add or Subtract from the Word

"If any man shall add... or take away... God shall take away his part..." – *Revelation 22:18–19*

B. Stay Awake and Alert

"Behold, I come as a thief. Blessed is he that watcheth..." – *Revelation 16:15*

C. Keep the Prophecy

"Blessed is he that keepeth the sayings of the prophecy of this book." – *Revelation 22:7*

28. Conclusion: Jesus Is the Center of Prophecy

All prophecy points to a Person—**Jesus Christ**.

"The testimony of Jesus is the spirit of prophecy." – *Revelation 19:10*

The end time message is not about charts and dates—it's about being ready to meet the **King**.

✦ Final Questions to Ask Ourselves:

Am I living in daily readiness for His return?

Is my name written in the Book of Life?

Am I warning others, preaching the gospel?

Am I walking in purity, filled with the Spirit?
Do I long for His appearing?

🔥 Final Prayer:

"Lord Jesus, keep me awake, holy, and burning with oil. I want to be found faithful when You return. Let me not be ashamed at Your coming. Make me ready. Use me in these last days to point others to You. Come, Lord Jesus."
– Amen.

Holy Spirit, Take Me Home

"For here have we no continuing city, but we seek one to come." **– Hebrews 13:14**

1. Introduction: The Cry of the Redeemed

In every child of God, there is a holy yearning for *home.* Not a physical house or place on earth, but that eternal presence of God where no sin, sorrow, or separation exists. This longing is not birthed by fear, but by love. It's the cry: **"Holy Spirit, take me home."**

This isn't a prayer for escape—but a surrender of heart. It's the desire to be fully led by the Holy Spirit, away from this world's corruption, and toward eternal fellowship with the Father.

"And grieve not the Holy Spirit of God, whereby ye are sealed unto the day of redemption." – *Ephesians 4:30*

2. The Holy Spirit: Our Comforter and Guide

Jesus promised the Holy Spirit would not leave us as orphans: **"And I will pray the Father, and He shall give you another Comforter, that He may abide with you forever."** – *John 14:16* The Holy Spirit does not just give power for service—He gives intimacy with God. He is our **guarantee**, our **seal**, and the very presence of heaven within. **"Now He which stablisheth us... and hath anointed us, is God; Who hath also sealed us, and given the earnest of the Spirit in** our hearts." – *2 Corinthians 1:21–22*

The word *"earnest"* here means **down payment**—the Holy Spirit is God's pledge that what He began in us will be finished in eternity.

3. This World is Not Our Home

Paul reminds us often that we are *strangers and pilgrims* here.

"For our conversation (citizenship) is in heaven; from whence also we look for the Saviour." – *Philippians 3:20*

"These all died in faith… and confessed that they were strangers and pilgrims on the earth." – *Hebrews 11:13*

The Holy Spirit stirs this truth daily in the believer's heart: *"Don't settle.*

Don't be conformed. Don't love the world." He keeps our eyes on eternity.
"Set your affection on things above, not on things on the earth." – *Colossians 3:2*

4. The Spirit Groans for Redemption

Creation groans. We groan. But also the Holy Spirit groans within us. **"Likewise the Spirit also helpeth our infirmities... but the Spirit itself maketh intercession for us with groanings which cannot be uttered."** – *Romans 8:26*
There is a yearning within that words cannot express—a longing

for the full redemption of our bodies.

"O wretched man that I am! who shall deliver me from the body of this death?" – *Romans 7:24*

"We ourselves... groan within ourselves, waiting for the adoption, to wit, the redemption of our body." – *Romans 8:23*

5. Led Homeward by the Spirit

The Holy Spirit is not merely a force; He is a Person, leading us step-by-step toward the Father.

"For as many as are led by the Spirit of God, they are the sons of God." – *Romans 8:14*

He leads us in holiness, in righteousness, and in love—never coercing, but always inviting us home.

He convicts (John 16:8), teaches (John 14:26), speaks (Revelation 2:7), and comforts (John 14:18). Every prompting of the Spirit points us to Jesus and prepares us for eternity.

6. Dying Daily to Live Eternally

To say "Holy Spirit, take me home" is not just about *going* home—but about *living* like we're already headed there.

"I die daily." – *1 Corinthians 15:31*
"If ye through the Spirit do mortify the deeds of the body, ye shall live." – *Romans 8:13*

Every time we choose Christ over self, we are being drawn nearer to

home. The Holy Spirit helps us crucify the flesh, reject sin, and walk in resurrection power.
"Walk in the Spirit, and ye shall not fulfil the lust of the flesh." – *Galatians 5:16*

7. The Spirit Prepares Us as the Bride

The Holy Spirit beautifies the Bride of Christ—making her ready.
"That He might sanctify and cleanse it with the washing of water by the word." – *Ephesians 5:26*
"And the Spirit and the bride say, Come." – *Revelation 22:17*
He prepares us not just for a place, but for a Person—for Jesus.

"Let us be glad and rejoice... for the marriage of the Lamb is come, and His wife hath made herself ready." – *Revelation 19:7* This readiness is the work of the Spirit in us. Without holiness, no man shall see the Lord (Hebrews 12:14), and the Spirit makes us holy.

8. Desiring to Depart and Be with Christ

Paul understood this cry:
"For to me to live is Christ, and to die is gain... having a desire to depart, and to be with Christ; which is far better." – *Philippians 1:21–23*

This was not escapism. Paul lived fully for Christ—but his heart longed to be with Jesus.

"We are confident, I say, and willing rather to be absent from the body, and to be present with the Lord." – *2 Corinthians 5:8*

9. The Eternal Home Promised

Jesus made a promise:

"In My Father's house are many mansions... I go to prepare a place for you... I will come again, and receive you unto Myself; that where I am, there ye may be also." – *John 14:2–3*

Our true home is not made with hands:

"For we know that if our earthly house... were dissolved, we have

a building of God, an house not made with hands, eternal in the heavens." – *2 Corinthians 5:1*

And it is the **Holy Spirit** who keeps us anchored to that hope.

10. Our Names Written in Heaven

Jesus told His disciples:

"Rejoice not, that the spirits are subject unto you; but rather rejoice, because your names are written in heaven." – *Luke 10:20*

The Holy Spirit is the witness:

"The Spirit itself beareth witness with our spirit, that we are the children of God." – *Romans 8:16*

He assures us daily: *You belong to God. You're going home.*

11. Yearning With Hope, Not Despair

"Looking for that blessed hope, and the glorious appearing of the great God and our Saviour Jesus Christ." – *Titus 2:13*

"Holy Spirit, take me home" is not a whisper of hopelessness—but a cry of **hope**.

The early church had a word: **Maranatha** – "The Lord is coming!" This hope kept them faithful, pure, and bold.

12. Until That Day...

Until that glorious day comes, the Holy Spirit is with us—empowering us to walk in love, truth, and light.

"Ye shall receive power, after that the Holy Ghost is come upon you: and ye shall be witnesses..."
– *Acts 1:8*
He is the down payment of the inheritance (Ephesians 1:14), the voice behind us (Isaiah 30:21), the oil in our lamps (Matthew 25:1–13).

13. A Prayer: Holy Spirit, Take Me Home

"Holy Spirit, take me home—not just one day when I die, but every day as I live. Lead me from the world's pull to heaven's peace. Sanctify me. Guide me. Seal me. Make me ready for Jesus. Make me love the Word, hunger for righteousness, and thirst for purity. Help me long for home—not out of fear, but out of fullness. Let me walk in holiness, led by You, until I hear the voice of the Bridegroom calling, 'Come up hither.'" – *Amen.*

14. Final Scriptures for Meditation

"He that shall endure unto the end, the same shall be saved." – *Matthew 24:13*

"Not by might, nor by power, but by My Spirit, saith the LORD." – *Zechariah 4:6*

"Grieve not the Holy Spirit of God, whereby ye are sealed unto the day of redemption." – *Ephesians 4:30*

"Now the Lord is that Spirit: and where the Spirit of the Lord is,

there is liberty." – *2 Corinthians 3:17*

"Even so, come, Lord Jesus." – *Revelation 22:20*

15. The Spirit and Our Daily Journey Toward Home

Each day on earth is one more step toward eternity. The Holy Spirit is not only the One who *seals* us for heaven, but the One who *sustains* us through the trials of life.

"The inward man is renewed day by day." – *2 Corinthians 4:16*

Even when the outer life is weary, broken, or persecuted, the Holy Spirit strengthens the inner life. He reminds us:

"This world is not your home. Keep going. Don't stop."
That constant inward renewal is the Spirit gently guiding us forward, reminding us that eternity is real and Jesus is worth it.

16. The Spirit and Suffering: Fuel for the Journey

In suffering, the Spirit becomes even more personal. When we suffer with Christ, the Spirit teaches us to long for the eternal home.
"If so be that we suffer with Him, that we may be also glorified together." – *Romans 8:17*
Paul continues:
"For I reckon that the sufferings of this present time are not

worthy to be compared with the glory which shall be revealed in us." – *Romans 8:18*

The Holy Spirit gives us the power to endure—not just to survive, but to thrive in faith, knowing that glory awaits.

17. What "Home" Really Means

When we say, **"Holy Spirit, take me home"**, what are we really longing for?

We're not asking to go to a place merely of rest or reward. We are asking to be fully **united with God**. That's the real home.

"In Thy presence is fullness of joy; at Thy right hand there are pleasures forevermore." – *Psalm 16:11*

"We shall be like Him; for we shall see Him as He is." – *1 John 3:2*

Heaven is not just about the absence of pain—it's about the presence of **Jesus**. And the Holy Spirit is the One who makes Jesus real to us even now (John 16:14). He whets our appetite for heaven by revealing the **beauty of Jesus**.

18. The Spirit Cries "Abba, Father"

The Holy Spirit does not teach us to long for a destination first—but for a **Father**.

"Ye have received the Spirit of adoption, whereby we cry, Abba, Father." – *Romans 8:15*

Home is not heaven without the Father.

This cry—"Abba, Father"—is not just words. It's a deep spiritual reality. It's the longing of a child for his Father's embrace. It's not fear of judgment, but **desire for closeness**.

That's why the Spirit leads us not only *to* holiness, but *into* intimacy.

19. A Spirit-Led Departure

For some, "Holy Spirit, take me home" will be a *final prayer*.

Whether quietly or suddenly, there will come a moment when the Spirit leads each believer to the presence of Jesus.

Stephen, the first Christian martyr, experienced this:

"But he, being full of the Holy Ghost, looked up stedfastly into

heaven, and saw the glory of God… and said, Lord Jesus, receive my spirit." – *Acts 7:55–59* Even in death, Stephen was not alone. The Holy Spirit filled him, opened his eyes, and *escorted* him home.

20. No More Separation

In heaven, the Spirit's inner witness will be replaced by **face-to-face fellowship**.
"Now we see through a glass, darkly; but then face to face." – *1 Corinthians 13:12* The longings will cease. The groanings will end. And the cry of "Take me home" will be met with Jesus saying:

"Well done... enter thou into the joy of thy Lord." – *Matthew 25:23*
The Holy Spirit's work in us will be complete. We will be glorified, transformed, and eternally alive in the presence of God.

21. Eternal Security in the Spirit

This entire journey is not held by our own strength, but by the faithfulness of God through His Spirit.
"He which hath begun a good work in you will perform it until the day of Jesus Christ." –
Philippians 1:6
"And grieve not the Holy Spirit of God, whereby ye are sealed unto the day of redemption." –
Ephesians 4:30

The Holy Spirit does not leave us halfway. He keeps us, teaches us, and strengthens us until we arrive safely home.

22. A Living Hope

Peter speaks of this hope: **"Blessed be the God and Father of our Lord Jesus Christ... which hath begotten us again unto a lively hope by the resurrection of Jesus Christ from the dead." –** *1 Peter 1:3*

This hope is not theory. It is **living** because Christ is risen, and the Holy Spirit makes Him alive in us. So we do not fear the end—we look forward to it with joy.

23. Our Heavenly Inheritance

"To an inheritance incorruptible, and undefiled, and that fadeth not away, reserved in heaven for you." – *1 Peter 1:4*

The Holy Spirit whispers daily: *"It's coming. Don't quit."*

Every promise is real. Every tear will be wiped. Every trial will be worth it.

"Eye hath not seen, nor ear heard... the things which God hath prepared for them that love Him. But God hath revealed them unto us by His Spirit." – *1 Corinthians 2:9–10*

24. Until We See His Face

This is the ultimate end of our journey:

"And they shall see His face; and His name shall be in their foreheads." – *Revelation 22:4*

The Spirit is preparing us for that **moment**. Nothing on earth can compare. No earthly glory or possession matters more.

We walk now by faith, by the Spirit. But soon, faith will turn to sight.

25. Final Thoughts: A Spirit-Filled Life Is a Homeward Life

To say "Holy Spirit, take me home" is to say:

I'm not living for this world.

I want to walk in holiness and intimacy.
I desire to see Jesus above all else.
I want the Spirit to lead me every day toward eternity.
"And Enoch walked with God: and he was not; for God took him." – *Genesis 5:24*
This is the goal: to walk so closely with God that one day the Spirit simply finishes the journey by taking us all the way *home*.

26. A Closing Benediction (Based on Scripture)

May the **grace of the Lord Jesus Christ**, and the **love of God**, and the **communion of the Holy Ghost**, be with you all (2

Corinthians 13:14). May you be led by the Spirit, walk in the Spirit, live in the Spirit. May your heart cry every day: "Holy Spirit, take me home," And may you be found faithful until that glorious day, When faith becomes sight, and sorrow becomes joy, And Jesus says, "Well done. Welcome home."

How to Reign with Christ

"If we suffer, we shall also reign with Him." – **2 Timothy 2:12**

1. Introduction: God's Eternal Purpose

God's plan has never been just to save people from sin—it has always been to raise them into **rulership** through His Son, Jesus Christ. From the beginning, mankind was created to reign.

"Let them have dominion..." – *Genesis 1:26*

Sin broke that dominion, but through Christ, dominion is restored. Salvation is the doorway; **reigning** is the destiny.

"And hast made us unto our God kings and priests: and we shall reign on the earth." – *Revelation 5:10*

To **reign with Christ** is not only a promise for the future—it's a call to live in spiritual authority today.

2. Reigning Is Promised to the Overcomer

Jesus made it plain that only those who **overcome** will reign with Him. **"To him that overcometh will I grant to sit with Me in My throne..."** – *Revelation 3:21* An overcomer is not someone who lives perfectly, but someone who endures faithfully, walking in the Spirit, and refusing to be overcome by the world. **"For whatsoever is born of God overcometh the world."** – *1 John 5:4*

3. Called to Rule with Christ

Jesus is not ruling alone—He is bringing many sons to glory

(Hebrews 2:10). The church is the **Bride of Christ**, but also the **co-heir** and **co-ruler** with Him.

"If we suffer, we shall also reign with Him..." – *2 Timothy 2:12*

"And he that overcometh... to him will I give power over the nations." – *Revelation 2:26*

Our calling is royal because Christ is a **King**, and we are in Him.

"The Spirit itself beareth witness... that we are the children of God... and joint-heirs with Christ." – *Romans 8:16–17*

4. How Do We Reign? A Step-by-Step Biblical Guide

Let's walk through the **biblical steps** that describe how to reign with Christ.

Step 1: Be Born of the Spirit

No one reigns with Christ unless they are **born again**.

"Except a man be born again, he cannot see the kingdom of God." – *John 3:3*

To reign with Christ, you must enter the kingdom—and that begins with **repentance and faith** in Jesus.

"That which is born of the flesh is flesh; and that which is born of the Spirit is spirit." – *John 3:6*

Step 2: Submit to the Rule of Christ Now

To reign *with* Christ, you must first be ruled *by* Christ.

"Why call ye Me, Lord, Lord, and do not the things which I say?" – *Luke 6:46*

Submission is the foundation. Jesus reigns through humility and obedience. So must we.

"Humble yourselves therefore under the mighty hand of God, that He may exalt you in due time." – *1 Peter 5:6*

Step 3: Walk in the Spirit

True reigning begins **within**. The Holy Spirit empowers you to overcome sin, fear, and the world. **"Walk in the Spirit, and ye shall not fulfil the lust of the flesh." –** *Galatians 5:16* Those who are Spirit-led are already operating under divine authority. **"For as many as are led by the Spirit of God, they are the sons of God." –** *Romans 8:14*

Step 4: Endure Suffering Faithfully

Suffering is not the enemy—it is the training ground for reigning. **"If we suffer, we shall also reign with Him." –** *2 Timothy 2:12*

"That ye may be counted worthy of the kingdom of God, for which ye also suffer." – *2 Thessalonians 1:5*

The cross comes before the crown. The fire of affliction purifies those who will share Christ's throne.

Step 5: Rule Over Sin and Flesh

Before we can be trusted to rule in eternity, we must rule our inner life.

"Let not sin therefore reign in your mortal body." – *Romans 6:12*

"He that ruleth his spirit is better than he that taketh a city." – *Proverbs 16:32*

This dominion is given **by the Spirit**, not by human strength.

Step 6: Serve as a Priest and King
We are called **kings and priests—**
to rule and intercede.
"But ye are a chosen generation, a royal priesthood…" – *1 Peter 2:9*
To reign is not to dominate—but to
serve with wisdom and prayer.
"The Son of man came not to be ministered unto, but to minister…" – *Matthew 20:28*

Step 7: Live for Eternity Now
Those who reign with Christ live
with heaven in mind.
"Set your affection on things above, not on things on the earth." – *Colossians 3:2*

"If ye then be risen with Christ, seek those things which are above." – *Colossians 3:1*
Living with eternity in focus prepares us for authority in the coming kingdom.

5. The Millennial Reign and Beyond
Scripture promises a literal reign of Christ on earth, where His saints will reign with Him.
"And they lived and reigned with Christ a thousand years." – *Revelation 20:4*
This is the **millennial kingdom**. Those who were faithful will rule cities, judge angels, and sit on thrones (Luke 19:17, 1 Corinthians 6:3).

6. Reigning Is Not for the Lukewarm

Jesus warned the lukewarm church: **"Because thou art lukewarm... I will spue thee out of My mouth."** *– Revelation 3:16*

Only the **overcomers**—those who walk in Spirit-led obedience—will sit with Him in His throne (Revelation 3:21).

Reigning is a reward for **faithful servants**, not for passive believers.

7. What We Will Reign Over

1. Sin – through the Spirit

"Sin shall not have dominion over you..." *– Romans 6:14*

2. Satan – under Jesus' authority

"I give you power… over all the power of the enemy." – *Luke 10:19*

3. Nations – in the millennial kingdom

"To him… will I give power over the nations." – *Revelation 2:26*

4. Angels – righteous judgment

"Know ye not that we shall judge angels?" – *1 Corinthians 6:3*

5. Creation – restoration of Eden-like dominion

"The creation waits for the sons of God…" – *Romans 8:19*

8. Reigning Now: Spiritual Authority

Even before eternity, believers walk in spiritual dominion. Jesus said:

"Behold, I give unto you power... over all the power of the enemy." – *Luke 10:19*

This power is not to exalt self, but to glorify Christ.

"The weapons of our warfare are not carnal, but mighty through God..." – *2 Corinthians 10:4*

9. Reigning Is Rooted in Love

Paul said:

"Faith which worketh by love." – *Galatians 5:6*

All authority in the kingdom flows through **love**. Without love, even great power is useless (1 Corinthians 13:1–3).
Those who reign with Christ must rule with His heart:
"He shall feed His flock like a shepherd..." – *Isaiah 40:11*

10. The Crowns of the Overcomer

The Bible speaks of **rewards and crowns** for those who endure:
Crown of life – for those who love Him (James 1:12)
Crown of righteousness – for those who long for His appearing (2 Timothy 4:8)
Crown of glory – for faithful shepherds (1 Peter 5:4)

Incorruptible crown – for self-control (1 Corinthians 9:25)
Crown of rejoicing – for soul winners (1 Thessalonians 2:19)
Each crown is a symbol of authority, awarded to those who lived for His kingdom.

11. Conclusion: Kings in Training

To reign with Christ is not automatic—it is **prepared** through obedience, suffering, and surrender.

"He that is faithful in that which is least is faithful also in much." – *Luke 16:10*

Jesus is preparing **a people** who reflect His character, walk in His Spirit, and love His appearing.

The question is not *"Will you go to heaven?"* but:
"Will you reign with Christ?"
"Be thou faithful unto death, and I will give thee a crown of life." – *Revelation 2:10*

Final Charge:
Let this be your prayer:
"Lord, train me. Break me. Fill me. Rule in me—so You may reign through me. I want to suffer with You now, so I can reign with You then. I want to overcome, not coast. I want to be found faithful when You come. Let me reign with You—not for glory, but because I love You."

The End Time – A Biblical Overview

1. Understanding the End Time

The "End Time" refers to the culmination of human history as revealed in the Bible. It is not a time of fear for believers, but a time of fulfillment and hope. Scripture gives us many insights, primarily through the teachings of Jesus, the prophets, and the apostles.

"Surely the Lord GOD will do nothing, but He revealeth His secret unto His servants the prophets." – *Amos 3:7*

2. Jesus' Teachings on the End

Jesus gives the most detailed account in **Matthew 24**, also echoed in **Mark 13** and **Luke 21**.

He described events that would mark the end:
Wars and rumors of wars
Famines and earthquakes
Persecution of believers
The rise of false prophets
The gospel preached in all the world

"And this gospel of the kingdom shall be preached in all the world for a witness unto all nations; and then shall the end come." – *Matthew 24:14*

3. Signs of the Times

Paul describes the moral and spiritual condition of humanity in the last days:

"This know also, that in the last days perilous times shall come.

For men shall be lovers of their own selves... having a form of godliness, but denying the power thereof." – *2 Timothy 3:1–5*

Jesus warned of deception:

"Take heed that no man deceive you." – *Matthew 24:4* **"For many shall come in My name, saying, I am Christ; and shall deceive many."** – *Matthew 24:5*

4. The Rise of Antichrist and Global Rebellion

The end times are marked by the rise of a final world leader known as the Antichrist or "man of sin":

"Let no man deceive you... that day shall not come, except there come a falling away first, and

that man of sin be revealed.” – *2 Thessalonians 2:3*

He will exalt himself above all that is called God:

“...who opposeth and exalteth himself above all that is called God... so that he as God sitteth in the temple of God, shewing himself that he is God.” – *2 Thessalonians 2:4*

5. The Great Tribulation

Jesus describes a time of unprecedented trouble:

“For then shall be great tribulation, such as was not since the beginning of the world... nor ever shall be.” – *Matthew 24:21*

This period will be marked by intense suffering, but it will be cut short for the sake of God's people: **"And except those days should be shortened, there should no flesh be saved: but for the elect's sake those days shall be shortened."** – *Matthew 24:22*

6. The Return of Christ

The return of Jesus is the central event of the end time. It will be visible, glorious, and unmistakable. **"For as the lightning cometh out of the east, and shineth even unto the west; so shall also the coming of the Son of man be."** – *Matthew 24:27*

"Behold, He cometh with clouds; and every eye shall see Him…" – *Revelation 1:7*

At this moment, Jesus will gather His people:

"And He shall send His angels with a great sound of a trumpet, and they shall gather together His elect from the four winds." – *Matthew 24:31*

7. The Resurrection and Rapture

Believers who died will rise first, and the living will be caught up:

"For the Lord Himself shall descend from heaven with a shout… and the dead in Christ shall rise first: then we which are alive… shall be caught up

together… to meet the Lord in the air." – *1 Thessalonians 4:16–17*
This is the hope of all believers, to be with Jesus forever.
"Wherefore comfort one another with these words." – *1 Thessalonians 4:18*

8. The Judgment
After His return, Jesus will judge the world.
"He hath appointed a day, in the which He will judge the world in righteousness by that man whom He hath ordained." – *Acts 17:31*
"For we must all appear before the judgment seat of Christ…" – *2 Corinthians 5:10*
Those who are written in the Book of Life will enter eternal life:

"And whosoever was not found written in the book of life was cast into the lake of fire." – *Revelation 20:15*

9. The New Heaven and New Earth

After judgment, God will make all things new:

"And I saw a new heaven and a new earth... And God shall wipe away all tears from their eyes." – *Revelation 21:1–4*

There will be no more death, sorrow, or pain. This is the eternal reward for the righteous.

"And there shall be no more curse: but the throne of God and of the Lamb shall be in it... and they shall reign forever and ever." – *Revelation 22:3–5*

10. How Should We Live?

Knowing these things, Scripture calls us to live holy, expectant lives. **"Seeing then that all these things shall be dissolved, what manner of persons ought ye to be in all holy conversation and godliness."** – *2 Peter 3:11*
"Watch therefore: for ye know not what hour your Lord doth come." – *Matthew 24:42*
"Blessed is that servant, whom his lord when he cometh shall find so doing." – *Matthew 24:46*

11. The Spirit and the Bride Say, Come

The final words of the Bible are an invitation and a promise:

"And the Spirit and the bride say, Come... And whosoever will, let him take the water of life freely." – *Revelation 22:17*

"Surely I come quickly. Amen. Even so, come, Lord Jesus." – *Revelation 22:20*

Conclusion

The end time is not a mystery for those who read the Bible. It's a period of great shaking and great hope. While the world descends into chaos, believers look up with

joy, knowing that Jesus is returning to restore all things. **"Lift up your heads; for your redemption draweth nigh."** – *Luke 21:28*
Stay alert. Stay faithful. Jesus is coming soon.

SIGNS OF THE END TIME: A BIBLICAL EXPLORATION

1. Introduction: God Reveals the End

The Bible declares that God never acts without revealing His plans: **"Surely the Lord GOD will do nothing, but He revealeth His**

secret unto His servants the prophets." – *Amos 3:7*

The "end time" refers to a specific season in God's plan, just before the return of Jesus Christ. It's not hidden or cryptic—Jesus, the prophets, and the apostles described the signs plainly, so that God's people would be prepared, not afraid.

2. Jesus' Master Prophecy: Matthew 24

The clearest and most comprehensive teaching on end time signs comes from Jesus Himself, especially in **Matthew 24**, often called the "Olivet Discourse."

"And as He sat upon the mount of Olives, the disciples came unto Him privately, saying, Tell us, when shall these things be? and what shall be the sign of Thy coming, and of the end of the world?" – *Matthew 24:3*

Jesus responds with detailed signs. Let's walk through them:

A. Deception Will Increase
"Take heed that no man deceive you." – *Matthew 24:4*
"For many shall come in My name, saying, I am Christ; and shall deceive many." – *Matthew 24:5*

Deception is the first warning. Spiritual confusion and false claims will abound. This includes false teachers, counterfeit prophets, and even false "christs."

B. Wars and Rumors of Wars
"And ye shall hear of wars and rumours of wars: see that ye be not troubled: for all these things must come to pass, but the end is not yet." – *Matthew 24:6*
This points to increasing global conflict, unrest, and instability. Jesus warned that these events would not mark the *end* yet, but would be *birth pains* (v. 8).

C. Natural Disasters and Famines
"For nation shall rise against nation... and there shall be famines, and pestilences, and

earthquakes, in divers places." – *Matthew 24:7*

Earthquakes, diseases, and famines—these signs occur worldwide and with increasing frequency. They serve as loud alarms for a world nearing climax.

D. Persecution of Believers

"Then shall they deliver you up to be afflicted, and shall kill you: and ye shall be hated of all nations for My name's sake." – *Matthew 24:9*

Christians will increasingly be opposed, marginalized, and even killed for their faith. The hatred isn't personal—it's for bearing the name of Jesus.

E. Love Will Grow Cold

"And because iniquity shall abound, the love of many shall wax cold." – *Matthew 24:12*
As sin increases, love—both for God and others—will decline. Society becomes more selfish, cruel, and indifferent to righteousness.

F. The Gospel Will Reach the World

"And this gospel of the kingdom shall be preached in all the world for a witness unto all nations; and then shall the end come." – *Matthew 24:14*
Despite the darkness, the gospel will shine globally. Every nation

will hear. The end comes only *after* this happens.

3. Paul's Prophetic Warnings

The apostle Paul echoes and expands on these themes in his letters. Let's look at key passages.

A. Perilous Times in the Last Days
"This know also, that in the last days perilous times shall come."
– 2 Timothy 3:1–5
Paul lists human behaviors that mark the last days:
Lovers of self
Lovers of money
Proud, arrogant, blasphemers
Disobedient to parents

Unthankful, unholy
Lovers of pleasure more than God
**"...Having a form of godliness,
but denying the power thereof:
from such turn away."** – *v. 5*
This isn't just about the world—but
about *religious people* who only
have a form of godliness. Paul
warns believers to separate from
such hypocrisy.

B. Doctrinal Apostasy
**"Now the Spirit speaketh
expressly, that in the latter times
some shall depart from the
faith..."** – *1 Timothy 4:1–2*
**"...giving heed to seducing
spirits, and doctrines of devils."**
A major sign is doctrinal
confusion—even *within* the church.

Strange teachings, spiritualism, legalism, and rebellion against truth will grow.

4. The Rise of the Antichrist

Another vital sign is the revealing of the "man of sin" or Antichrist. **"Let no man deceive you... that day shall not come, except there come a falling away first, and that man of sin be revealed." –** *2 Thessalonians 2:3*

He will:

Oppose all that is called God (v. 4)

Sit in the temple, claiming to be God

Come with power, signs, and lying wonders (v. 9)

His coming is a final test for those who refuse truth:

"And for this cause God shall send them strong delusion, that they should believe a lie." – *v. 11*

5. The Rebirth of Israel

Biblically, Israel plays a central role in end-time prophecy. Jesus speaks of it symbolically:

"Now learn a parable of the fig tree... when his branch is yet tender... ye know that summer is nigh." – *Matthew 24:32–33*

Israel is often represented as a fig tree in the Bible. Its rebirth as a nation in 1948 is seen by many as a major prophetic milestone.

6. Technology, Control, and the Mark

Revelation gives chilling details about global control in the last days:

"...no man might buy or sell, save he that had the mark..." – *Revelation 13:17*

The "mark of the beast" will be required for all commerce. This implies:

A global economy

A surveillance/control system

A unified political and religious structure

"And he causeth all, both small and great, rich and poor... to receive a mark." – *Revelation 13:16*

Such a system was unimaginable in John's day—but is now technologically possible.

7. The Days of Noah and Lot

Jesus compares the end times to two biblical periods:

"But as the days of Noah were, so shall also the coming of the Son of man be." – *Matthew 24:37*

"Likewise also as it was in the days of Lot..." – *Luke 17:28*

In Noah's day:

Violence filled the earth (Genesis 6:11)

People ignored God's warnings

Society was obsessed with daily pleasure (eating, drinking, marrying)

In Lot's day:

Immorality and perversion were rampant (Genesis 19)
People continued life as usual, unaware of pending judgment
Jesus says *this* is the attitude of the last generation.

8. Scoffing and Denial

Peter warns that in the end times, people will mock the idea of judgment.

"Knowing this first, that there shall come in the last days scoffers... saying, Where is the promise of His coming?" – *2 Peter 3:3–4*

They'll claim the world has always been the same, denying God's intervention. But Peter reminds us:

"The Lord is not slack concerning His promise…" – *v. 9*
God delays only to give people more time to repent.

9. Worldwide Lawlessness and Rebellion

Jesus said:
"And because iniquity shall abound, the love of many shall wax cold." – *Matthew 24:12*
Paul echoes this:
"…that man of sin… the mystery of iniquity doth already work." – *2 Thessalonians 2:3–7*
Rebellion against all forms of godly order will rise:
Against family
Against biblical marriage

Against government (Romans 13)
Against spiritual authority

10. The Harvest Is Ready

In **Matthew 13**, Jesus uses a parable to explain the end time: **"The harvest is the end of the world; and the reapers are the angels."** – *Matthew 13:39*
The wheat (God's people) and the tares (false believers) grow together. At the end, there's a separation.

11. The Final Call: Be Watchful

Jesus constantly urges readiness:

"Watch therefore: for ye know not what hour your Lord doth come." – *Matthew 24:42*
"Be ye also ready: for in such an hour as ye think not the Son of man cometh." – *Matthew 24:44*
"Blessed is that servant, whom his lord when he cometh shall find so doing." – *Matthew 24:46*
The greatest danger is not global events—it's spiritual sleep.

12. Summary of End Time Signs (Scripture-Focused)

Sign
Scripture Reference
Deception and false christs

Matthew 24:4–5

Wars and rumors of wars

Matthew 24:6

Famines and earthquakes

Matthew 24:7

Persecution of Christians

Matthew 24:9

Apostasy and false teaching

1 Timothy 4:1, 2 Thessalonians 2:3

Increase of wickedness

Matthew 24:12

Gospel to all nations

Matthew 24:14

Scoffers and mockers

2 Peter 3:3–4

Rebirth of Israel

Matthew 24:32–34 (parable of the fig tree)
Mark of the beast
Revelation 13:16–17
Days of Noah and Lot
Luke 17:26–30
Strong delusion
2 Thessalonians 2:11

13. Closing: Jesus Is Coming

The signs are not meant to scare, but to prepare. Every fulfilled prophecy confirms God's Word is true.
"Heaven and earth shall pass away, but My words shall not pass away." – *Matthew 24:35*

And the last promise of the Bible is clear:

"Surely I come quickly. Amen. Even so, come, Lord Jesus." – *Revelation 22:20*

Abiding in Christ: Living in Deep Fellowship with Jesus

Introduction

In a world filled with hurry, distraction, and spiritual dryness, the call to **abide in Christ** offers a life-giving alternative. Abiding in Christ is not just a lofty spiritual concept—it is the heartbeat of true discipleship. Jesus Himself described it as the key to bearing fruit, walking in peace, and experiencing the fullness of life.

In **John 15:4**, Jesus says:

"Abide in Me, and I in you. As the branch cannot bear fruit by itself, unless it abides in the vine, neither can you, unless you abide in Me." This invitation is both simple and profound. To **abide** means to dwell, remain, or stay connected. It is an ongoing relationship of dependence, obedience, and intimacy with Christ.

This essay explores what it means to abide in Christ, why it matters, how it transforms every area of life, and how believers can live in constant fellowship with Him.

1. What Does It Mean to Abide in Christ?

A. The Word "Abide" Defined

The Greek word for abide in John 15 is **"menō"**, which means:
To remain
To stay
To dwell
To continue
It implies **permanence** and **closeness**. Abiding is not a once-a-week experience or emotional moment; it is the **ongoing condition of the believer's heart**.

B. Abiding Is Relationship, Not Religion

Abiding in Christ is not about following a set of rules—it's about **walking with a person**. It is a moment-by-moment relationship with Jesus where we:
Trust Him

Listen to Him
Obey Him
Rest in Him
Abiding is living in constant union
with Jesus, drawing our strength,
wisdom, and identity from Him.

2. The Biblical Foundation of
Abiding

**A. John 15 – The Vine and the
Branches**
This chapter is the central teaching
on abiding. Jesus uses the metaphor
of a vine and branches to describe
our connection to Him.
Jesus is the true vine
The Father is the gardener
We are the branches
John 15:5:

"Whoever abides in Me and I in him, he it is that bears much fruit, for apart from Me you can do nothing."

The message is clear: **apart from abiding in Christ, we can do nothing of eternal value.**

B. Other Key Scriptures on Abiding

1 John 2:6 – *"Whoever says he abides in Him ought to walk in the same way in which He walked."*

Colossians 2:6–7 – *"Therefore, as you received Christ Jesus the Lord, so walk in Him, rooted and built up in Him..."*

Galatians 2:20 – *"It is no longer I who live, but Christ who lives in me..."*

These passages reinforce that abiding means **living a life that reflects Jesus**.

3. Why Abiding in Christ Matters

A. It's the Source of Spiritual Life

Just as a branch cannot survive apart from the vine, we cannot thrive spiritually without constant connection to Christ.

Abiding brings nourishment

Abiding brings spiritual vitality

Abiding keeps us alive in Christ

B. It's the Key to Fruitfulness

John 15:8:

"By this my Father is glorified, that you bear much fruit and so prove to be my disciples."

Fruitfulness in the Christian life—
love, joy, peace, patience, impact—
flows not from effort, but from
connection.
We bear fruit by:
Being rooted in God's Word
Walking in the Spirit
Living in obedience

C. It's the Foundation for Peace and Joy
John 15:11:
"These things I have spoken to you,
that My joy may be in you, and that
your joy may be full."
When we abide, we experience
sustained joy—not based on
circumstances, but on the presence
of Christ.
Isaiah 26:3:

"You will keep in perfect peace those whose minds are steadfast, because they trust in You."

D. It's Essential for Endurance

Life is full of challenges. Abiding gives us the strength to endure hardship, resist temptation, and remain faithful through trials.
Psalm 91:1:
"Whoever dwells in the shelter of the Most High will rest in the shadow of the Almighty."

4. How to Abide in Christ Daily

Abiding is a daily choice—a lifestyle cultivated by spiritual disciplines and intentional living.

A. Abide Through the Word

John 15:7:
"If you abide in Me, and My words abide in you…"
Letting God's Word dwell in us is a major way we stay connected to Jesus.
Read the Bible daily
Meditate on Scripture
Apply the Word to your life
Psalm 1:2–3 compares a person who delights in God's Word to a tree planted by streams of water.

B. Abide Through Prayer

Prayer is ongoing communication with Christ. Not just asking for things—but listening, worshiping, and being still in His presence.
1 Thessalonians 5:17:
"Pray without ceasing."

Through prayer, we invite Christ into every area of life.

C. Abide Through Obedience
John 15:10:
"If you keep My commandments, you will abide in My love..."
Obedience is not burdensome—it's the **natural expression of love and trust**.
1 John 5:3:
"In fact, this is love for God: to keep His commands."
When we obey God, we remain close to Him.

D. Abide Through the Holy Spirit
The Holy Spirit makes the presence of Jesus real in our lives. He

empowers us to stay connected, to grow, and to bear fruit.

John 14:16–17:

"I will ask the Father, and He will give you another Helper... the Spirit of truth..."

To abide, we must walk **in step with the Spirit** (Galatians 5:25).

E. Abide Through Worship and Gratitude

Worship re-centers our hearts. Gratitude shifts our focus from problems to promises.

Hebrews 13:15:

"Let us continually offer to God a sacrifice of praise..."

Worship is not just music—it's a lifestyle of exalting Christ.

5. The Fruit of Abiding in Christ

Jesus promises that abiding will produce **fruit**—visible evidence of His life in us.

A. The Fruit of the Spirit
Galatians 5:22–23:
"But the fruit of the Spirit is love, joy, peace, patience, kindness…"
These qualities grow as we remain in Christ.

B. The Fruit of Influence
As we abide, we become a light to others. Our lives point people to Jesus through:
Godly character
Wise counsel
Acts of love and service

John 15:16:
"I chose you and appointed you that you should go and bear fruit—fruit that will last."

C. The Fruit of Answered Prayer
John 15:7:
"Ask whatever you wish, and it will be done for you."
When we abide, our desires align with God's will—and our prayers become powerful and effective.

6. Hindrances to Abiding
Abiding is a spiritual discipline that requires guarding against distractions and spiritual drift.
A. Sin and Disobedience
Isaiah 59:2:

"Your iniquities have separated you from your God..."
Sin disrupts our fellowship with Christ. Confession and repentance restore it (1 John 1:9).

B. Busyness and Distraction
Luke 10:41:
"Martha, Martha... you are worried and upset about many things."
We can be so busy doing "good things" that we neglect the **best thing**—abiding in Christ.

C. Self-Reliance
John 15:5:
"Apart from Me, you can do nothing."

Pride and self-sufficiency hinder abiding. We must daily depend on Christ, not ourselves.

7. Abiding in Seasons of Suffering

Abiding becomes especially powerful in hardship. Trials test our faith—but they also deepen our roots.

A. Abiding Brings Comfort

2 Corinthians 1:3–4:

"The God of all comfort... comforts us in all our troubles..."

Christ abides with us **in the fire**—like He did with Shadrach, Meshach, and Abednego (Daniel 3).

B. Abiding Strengthens Endurance

James 1:12:
"Blessed is the one who perseveres under trial…"
When we abide, we don't just survive—we grow stronger, more resilient, more Christlike.

C. Abiding Produces Intimacy
Psalm 34:18:
"The Lord is close to the brokenhearted…"
Suffering can strip away distractions and drive us into **deeper communion with Christ**.

8. Abiding in Community
Abiding in Christ is personal, but not private. We need the **body of Christ** to help us grow.

Fellowship encourages abiding (Hebrews 10:25)
Accountability sustains it
Worship magnifies it
Shared mission spreads it
Jesus calls us not just to abide **in Him**, but to love **one another** (John 15:12).

9. Abiding for a Lifetime

Abiding is not seasonal—it is **for life**.
1 John 2:28:
"And now, dear children, continue in Him, so that when He appears we may be confident..."
The reward of abiding is not just for today—it is **eternal life**.
Revelation 3:20–21:

"To the one who is victorious, I will give the right to sit with Me on My throne…"

Conclusion: Make Abiding Your Way of Life

To abide in Christ is to live in **constant fellowship** with the One who loves you, saved you, and sustains you. It is the secret to joy, power, peace, and spiritual fruitfulness. It is not always easy, but it is always worth it.

Jesus invites you—not to visit occasionally—but to **dwell continually**.

So today, let this be your prayer: **"Lord, help me to remain in You—when it's easy and when**

it's hard. Let Your Word abide in me. Let Your Spirit lead me. Let my life bear fruit that brings You glory. Teach me to abide."
Because when you **abide in Christ**, you live the life you were always created for.

Living for Christ: A Life of Purpose, Power, and Surrender

Introduction

To live for Christ is not simply to admire Him, believe in Him, or occasionally follow His teachings. It is to **die to self and fully surrender** every part of one's life to His lordship. Living for Christ means walking in relationship with Him, aligning with His will, bearing

His image, and fulfilling His mission.

In a world where so many live for pleasure, popularity, or possessions, Christ calls His followers to a higher path—one that is marked by love, sacrifice, obedience, and eternal purpose. This essay explores what it truly means to live for Christ, why it matters, and how to walk out this call every day.

1. The Call to Live for Christ

A. Biblical Foundation

Paul summarizes the Christian life in Galatians 2:20:

"I have been crucified with Christ and I no longer live, but Christ lives in me. The life I now live in the body,

I live by faith in the Son of God, who loved me and gave himself for me."
To live for Christ begins with **dying to self**. It's a radical reorientation—from self-centered living to Christ-centered living.
Jesus Himself said in **Luke 9:23**: *"Whoever wants to be my disciple must deny themselves and take up their cross daily and follow me."*
Living for Christ is not a one-time decision—it is a daily surrender.

B. Why We Live for Christ
Because He Died for Us 2 Corinthians 5:15 – *"He died for all, that those who live should no longer live for themselves but for him who died for them..."*

Because We Belong to Him 1 Corinthians 6:19–20 – *"You are not your own; you were bought at a price..."*
Because He Lives in Us Colossians 1:27 – *"Christ in you, the hope of glory."*

2. The Characteristics of a Life Lived for Christ

A. A Life of Surrender
Surrender is not weakness—it's the **gateway to spiritual power**. When we lay down our will, God fills us with His.
Romans 12:1:
"Offer your bodies as a living sacrifice, holy and pleasing to God..."

Living for Christ requires surrendering:
Our desires
Our plans
Our time
Our resources
Our reputation
This surrender is not out of fear but out of love for the One who gave everything for us.

B. A Life of Obedience
John 14:15 – *"If you love me, keep my commandments."*
Obedience is not legalism—it is love in action. Living for Christ means **obeying His Word** even when it's unpopular or costly. Jesus doesn't ask for part of our obedience—He asks for all of it.

C. A Life of Holiness

1 Peter 1:16 – *"Be holy, because I am holy."*

Holiness is not perfection but **being set apart**. Living for Christ means rejecting sin, resisting temptation, and pursuing purity in heart, mind, and action.

D. A Life of Love

John 13:35 – *"By this everyone will know that you are my disciples, if you love one another."*

To live for Christ is to **love like Christ**—selflessly, sacrificially, and without condition.

This love extends to:

Friends and family

Strangers
Enemies
The marginalized and broken

E. A Life of Purpose

Living for Christ means discovering and walking in the **purpose** He designed for you.

Ephesians 2:10 – *"For we are God's handiwork, created in Christ Jesus to do good works…"*

Your gifts, passions, and experiences are tools for God's glory.

3. The Cost of Living for Christ

Jesus never sugar-coated the cost. In fact, He told His followers to **count the cost** (Luke 14:28–33).

A. Dying to Self

Living for Christ means daily crucifying the flesh—its desires, pride, and ego. It may mean giving up certain habits, relationships, or ambitions.

Galatians 5:24 – *"Those who belong to Christ Jesus have crucified the flesh..."*

B. Facing Persecution

2 Timothy 3:12 – *"Everyone who wants to live a godly life in Christ Jesus will be persecuted."*

The world rejected Jesus—and it may reject those who follow Him. But Jesus said: *"Rejoice, because great is your reward in heaven."* (Matthew 5:12)

C. Being Misunderstood

Living for Christ may mean being **misunderstood** or mocked. But we must choose God's approval over man's.

Galatians 1:10 – *"Am I trying to please people? If I were still trying to please people, I would not be a servant of Christ."*

4. The Joy of Living for Christ

Despite the cost, living for Christ is not a burden—it is the **most joyful, fulfilling life possible**.

A. Joy in His Presence

Psalm 16:11 – *"In your presence there is fullness of joy…"*

When we live for Christ, we experience a **deep, sustaining joy** that circumstances can't take away.

B. Peace in the Storm

Philippians 4:7 – *"The peace of God... will guard your hearts and your minds in Christ Jesus."*

Living for Christ doesn't exempt us from storms, but it does give us **peace within them.**

C. Confidence in Eternity

John 14:2–3 – *"I go to prepare a place for you... I will come again and take you to myself."*

Living for Christ means we don't fear death—we look forward to eternity.

5. How to Live for Christ Daily

A. Spend Time with Him

John 15:4 – *"Abide in Me, and I in you..."*

You can't live for someone you don't spend time with. Make prayer and Scripture a **daily priority**.

B. Follow His Word

Psalm 119:105 – *"Your word is a lamp to my feet..."*

God's Word is your **guide**. Read it, study it, live it.

C. Be Led by the Spirit

Romans 8:14 – *"For those who are led by the Spirit of God are the children of God."*

Ask the Holy Spirit to guide your thoughts, decisions, and actions.

D. Stay in Fellowship

Hebrews 10:25 – *"Do not give up meeting together..."*

The Christian life is not meant to be lived alone. Surround yourself with other believers for support and accountability.

E. Serve Others
Mark 10:45 – *"The Son of Man did not come to be served, but to serve..."*
Look for ways to use your time and talents to bless others.

6. Living for Christ in a Fallen World
A. Standing Firm
1 Corinthians 16:13 – *"Be on your guard; stand firm in the faith; be courageous; be strong."*
The culture may oppose Christian values, but we are called to **stand firm**—with grace and truth.
B. Being a Light
Matthew 5:14 – *"You are the light of the world..."*

Your life should reflect Christ so brightly that others are drawn to Him.

7. Living for Christ in Suffering

Pain has a way of refining faith. Paul said in Philippians 1:21:

"For to me, to live is Christ and to die is gain."

Even in suffering, our lives can glorify Christ. Like Paul in prison, like Job in loss, or like Jesus on the cross, we can suffer with **purpose and power**.

2 Corinthians 4:17:

"Our light and momentary troubles are achieving for us an eternal glory..."

8. Living for Christ and Making Disciples

Matthew 28:19 – *"Go and make disciples of all nations…"*

Living for Christ includes **leading others to Him**. Share your testimony. Speak truth. Love deeply. Let your life be a living invitation to Christ.

9. Living for Christ Until the End

Revelation 2:10 – *"Be faithful, even to the point of death, and I will give you the crown of life."*

Living for Christ is not just about starting well—it's about **finishing strong**. Stay faithful. Keep running. Your reward awaits.

Conclusion: The Life You Were Made For

Living for Christ is not a restriction—it is a **release into your true identity and purpose**. It is the most meaningful, powerful, and rewarding life possible. It means waking up every day with eternal significance, knowing you are loved, led, and sent by the King of kings.

If you've drifted, come back. If you've been lukewarm, recommit. If you're hurting, let Christ carry you. If you're strong, press in deeper. Because nothing compares to a life fully surrendered—fully alive—**fully for Christ**.

"Whatever you do, whether in word or deed, do it all in the name of the Lord Jesus." (Colossians 3:17)

Live for Him. Live through Him.
Live with Him.
Live for Christ.

Hope in Hard Times: Holding On
When Life Hurts

Introduction

Hard times are inevitable. Whether
it's a personal loss, a financial crisis,
a health battle, or a season of
spiritual dryness, life brings
seasons where pain feels
overwhelming and the future
seems uncertain. In those moments,
hope becomes more than just a
comforting word—it becomes a
lifeline.

Hope in hard times is not wishful
thinking or naive optimism. It is the
confident expectation that, despite

how things look or feel, God is present, His promises are true, and better days are coming. The Bible is full of stories and truths that offer real hope for real people facing real struggles.

In this essay, we will explore what hope truly is, where it comes from, why it matters, and how to nurture it when life is at its hardest.

1. What Is Hope?

A. Biblical Definition of Hope

Hope, in the Bible, is not the same as mere optimism or positivity. The world defines hope as a desire for something good to happen—with no guarantee. For example: *"I hope things get better."*

But biblical hope is **confident expectation**. It is rooted in God's unchanging character and promises. **Hebrews 6:19** describes hope as:

"an anchor for the soul, firm and secure."

It is not anchored in feelings or circumstances but in **God Himself**.

2. Why We Need Hope in Hard Times

A. Hard Times Are Inevitable
Jesus said in **John 16:33**:

"In this world you will have trouble. But take heart! I have overcome the world."

Suffering is part of the human experience. No one is exempt. The presence of hard times is not a sign of God's absence. Instead, it's in those seasons that **hope becomes essential**.

B. Without Hope, People Perish

Proverbs 13:12 says:

"Hope deferred makes the heart sick..."

When hope is lost, despair sets in. Depression, fear, and hopelessness can lead people to give up on themselves, others, and even life. This is why nurturing hope is **not optional**—it's **life-saving**.

3. Sources of Hope

A. God's Word

The Bible is a wellspring of hope. Romans 15:4 says:

"Everything that was written in the past was written to teach us, so that through the endurance taught in the Scriptures and the encouragement they provide we might have hope." God's Word reminds us of His faithfulness, love, and power in every generation. When we read the stories of Job, David, Joseph, and Paul, we see that trials don't have the final say—**God does**.

B. God's Promises

God is a promise-keeper. His promises are **yes and amen** in Christ (2 Corinthians 1:20). Holding onto His promises gives us strength to endure.

Here are a few promises that restore hope:

Isaiah 41:10 – *"Do not fear, for I am with you..."*

Romans 8:28 – *"God works all things together for good..."*
Jeremiah 29:11 – *"Plans to prosper you, not to harm you..."*

C. The Holy Spirit

Romans 15:13 says:

"May the God of hope fill you with all joy and peace... so that you may overflow with hope by the power of the Holy Spirit."

Hope is not self-generated. It is a fruit of the Holy Spirit working in us. Even when we feel weak, the Spirit strengthens our inner man to believe again.

4. Biblical Examples of Hope in Hard Times

A. Job: Hope in Suffering

Job lost everything—children, health, wealth—yet declared: *"Though he slay me, yet will I hope in him."* (Job 13:15) Job's story reminds us that **our circumstances don't cancel God's love or plan**. In the end, God restored him double.

B. Joseph: Hope in Injustice

Betrayed by his brothers, sold as a slave, falsely accused, and imprisoned—Joseph had every reason to give up. But he trusted God. Later he said: *"You meant evil against me, but God meant it for good."* (Genesis 50:20) God used Joseph's pain to elevate him to purpose.

C. David: Hope in the Wilderness

Before becoming king, David spent years fleeing from Saul. In the caves and deserts, he wrote psalms of lament and hope:

"Why, my soul, are you downcast?... Put your hope in God." (Psalm 42:11)

David teaches us to **speak hope to our own souls**.

5. What Hope Does in Our Lives

A. Hope Anchors Us

Hebrews 6:19:

"We have this hope as an anchor for the soul, firm and secure."

In storms, hope keeps us from drifting. It stabilizes our faith and emotions.

B. Hope Strengthens Us

Isaiah 40:31:

"Those who hope in the Lord will renew their strength..."

Hope gives us the ability to endure long seasons of waiting, suffering, or silence.

C. Hope Purifies Us

1 John 3:3:

"All who have this hope in him purify themselves, just as he is pure."

Hope in Christ's return motivates us to live holy lives.

6. How to Cultivate Hope in Hard Times

A. Stay Rooted in God's Word

God's Word is a seed of hope. Read the Bible daily. Meditate on it. Memorize promises.

Psalm 119:114:

"You are my refuge and my shield; I have put my hope in your word."

B. Surround Yourself with Encouragement

Hope thrives in the company of faith-filled people. Avoid toxic negativity. Listen to sermons, worship, and testimonies.

Hebrews 10:23–25:

"Let us hold unswervingly to the hope we profess... encouraging one another."

C. Pray Honestly and Persistently

Pour out your heart to God. Lament is not a lack of faith—it's the language of the hurting.

Romans 12:12:

"Be joyful in hope, patient in affliction, faithful in prayer."

D. Recall God's Faithfulness

Remember past victories. Keep a "hope journal" of answered prayers and miracles.

Lamentations 3:21–23:

"Yet this I call to mind and therefore I have hope: Because of the Lord's great love we are not consumed..."

E. Serve Others

Serving shifts your focus. It reminds you that you're not alone, and it releases the joy of giving.

2 Corinthians 1:4:

"[God] comforts us... so that we can comfort those in any trouble..."

7. Hope and Waiting

Waiting is one of the hardest parts of life—and one of the most powerful tests of hope.

Psalm 130:5:

"I wait for the Lord, my whole being waits, and in his word I put my hope."

God is never late. His delays are not His denials. While you wait:
Keep worshiping
Keep obeying
Keep believing
Isaiah 30:18:
"The Lord longs to be gracious to you... Blessed are all who wait for him!"

8. The Difference Between Hope and Denial

Hope is not denial. Hope doesn't pretend everything is okay. It acknowledges the pain while **clinging to truth**.
David didn't deny his fears—he processed them **through** faith.
Jesus Himself wept at Lazarus'

tomb, even though He knew
resurrection was coming.
Hope says:
"It hurts—but God is with me."
*"I don't understand—but I trust
Him."*
*"It's not over—God is still writing my
story."*

9. Hope in Jesus Christ

Ultimately, true hope is not in
things getting better—it's in **Jesus
Himself**.
Titus 2:13 calls Him:
*"our blessed hope—the appearing of
the glory of our great God and
Savior, Jesus Christ."*
Our hope is:
Not in our ability, but in His
faithfulness

Not in the outcome, but in His presence
Not in the timeline, but in His sovereignty
Colossians 1:27:
"Christ in you, the hope of glory."

10. Final Encouragement: Hold On
Whatever you're facing today, know this:
You are not alone.
God sees, knows, and cares.
He is still in control.
Your pain has purpose.
And hope is **alive**—because Jesus is alive.
Romans 5:5:
"And hope does not disappoint us, because God's love has been poured

out into our hearts through the Holy Spirit."

Conclusion: Hope Is a Choice and a Gift

Hope in hard times is both **a decision and a grace**. We choose to hope, and God gives us the strength to keep choosing—even when it's hard. It's okay to feel weary. It's okay to cry. But don't give up.
God is not finished.
Your story is not over.
And your future is still full of promise—because your hope is not in what you see, but in the God who **sees you**.

So today, whisper it out loud: **"I will hope in God."**

The Power and Purpose of Prayer
Introduction
Prayer is one of the most essential and transformative aspects of the Christian life. It is not just a religious ritual or a spiritual duty— it is a lifeline to God, a divine conversation, and a sacred space where heaven meets earth. Through prayer, we connect with our Creator, align ourselves with His will, and experience the power and presence of the Holy Spirit. Yet for many believers, prayer remains a mystery or a struggle.
What is prayer, really? Why is it so powerful? And how can we

cultivate a deeper and more effective prayer life?

This essay explores the biblical foundation of prayer, its various forms, its power in both personal and corporate life, and practical ways to strengthen your prayer life today.

1. What Is Prayer?

Prayer is, simply put, **communion with God**. It is speaking with—and listening to—our Heavenly Father. It is an act of worship, dependence, and relationship. It reflects a heart that seeks God's presence, guidance, intervention, and fellowship.

Prayer is not a performance. It's not about eloquent words or religious

repetition. Jesus warned against empty phrases in Matthew 6:7: *"When you pray, do not keep on babbling like pagans, for they think they will be heard because of their many words."*
True prayer comes from a heart that is humble, honest, and hungry for God.

2. The Biblical Foundation of Prayer

Prayer is woven throughout the Bible—from Genesis to Revelation. It is the thread that connects God's people with His presence, promises, and purposes.
In the Old Testament, we see Abraham interceding for Sodom

(Genesis 18), Moses pleading for Israel (Exodus 32), David pouring out his heart in the Psalms, and Elijah calling down fire from heaven (1 Kings 18).

In the New Testament, Jesus models a life of constant prayer (Mark 1:35), teaches His disciples how to pray (Matthew 6:9-13), and prays fervently before His crucifixion (Luke 22:42). The early Church was born in a prayer meeting (Acts 1:14) and sustained by continual prayer.

Throughout Scripture, prayer is portrayed not as an optional discipline but as an essential part of knowing God and fulfilling His will.

3. Why Prayer Is Powerful

Prayer is powerful because it connects us to **the all-powerful God**. When we pray, we are not just sending thoughts into the universe—we are speaking to the Creator and Sustainer of all things.

a. Prayer Changes Us

Prayer is not only about changing our circumstances—it changes **us**. In the process of prayer, our hearts are softened, our minds are renewed, and our desires are aligned with God's will.

Romans 12:2 reminds us to be transformed by the renewing of our minds, and prayer is a key way that happens.

b. Prayer Moves Heaven

James 5:16 says:

"The effective, fervent prayer of a righteous man avails much."
God responds to the prayers of His people. History is filled with examples of how prayer has led to revivals, miracles, healing, deliverance, and divine intervention.

c. Prayer Invites God's Will
Jesus taught us to pray, *"Your kingdom come, Your will be done on earth as it is in heaven."* (Matthew 6:10)
When we pray according to God's will, we become **partners with Him in accomplishing His purposes on the earth**.

4. Types of Prayer

There are many types of prayer, each serving a unique purpose in our relationship with God.

a. Worship and Adoration

This kind of prayer focuses on **who God is** rather than what He does. It is the highest form of prayer, as it places God at the center of our hearts.

Example: "Holy, holy, holy is the Lord God Almighty..." (Revelation 4:8)

b. Thanksgiving

This prayer expresses **gratitude** for God's blessings, both big and small. A thankful heart opens the door to more of God's presence.

1 Thessalonians 5:18: *"Give thanks in all circumstances..."*

c. Confession and Repentance

Honest confession is vital for spiritual health. When we confess our sins, God is faithful to forgive and cleanse us (1 John 1:9). Psalm 51 is a powerful example of David's prayer of repentance.

d. Supplication (Petition)

This is asking God for our personal needs—spiritual, emotional, physical, or financial.

Philippians 4:6: *"Do not be anxious about anything, but in every situation, by prayer and petition, present your requests to God."*

e. Intercession

Intercessory prayer is praying on behalf of others. It is a powerful expression of love and spiritual warfare.

Ezekiel 22:30: *"I looked for someone among them who would stand in the gap..."*

f. Listening Prayer

Prayer is not just speaking—it's also **hearing**. Learning to recognize God's voice comes through stillness, Scripture, and practice. John 10:27: *"My sheep listen to my voice..."*

5. Barriers to Effective Prayer

While God desires to answer our prayers, there are factors that can hinder our communication with Him.

a. Unconfessed Sin

Psalm 66:18 says:

"If I had cherished sin in my heart, the Lord would not have listened."

b. Unforgiveness
Mark 11:25:
"When you stand praying, if you hold anything against anyone, forgive them..."
Unforgiveness blocks God's grace and hinders our prayers.

c. Doubt and Unbelief
James 1:6-7 warns that those who doubt "should not expect to receive anything from the Lord."
Faith is the key that unlocks heaven's response.

6. Jesus' Teachings on Prayer

Jesus is the ultimate model of a powerful prayer life. His teachings and example provide deep insight into how we should pray.

a. The Lord's Prayer

Found in Matthew 6:9-13, this model prayer includes:

Worship: "Our Father in heaven, hallowed be Your name"

Surrender: "Your kingdom come, Your will be done..."

Dependence: "Give us this day our daily bread"

Forgiveness: "Forgive us our debts..."

Protection: "Deliver us from evil"

b. Private and Sincere Prayer

Matthew 6:6:

"But when you pray, go into your room, close the door and pray to your Father..."

True prayer is intimate, not performative.

7. The Role of the Holy Spirit in Prayer

The Holy Spirit is central to a vibrant prayer life. He helps us pray according to God's will and empowers us beyond our human limitations.

Romans 8:26:

"We do not know what we ought to pray for, but the Spirit Himself intercedes for us..."

The Spirit also:

Helps us pray in tongues (1 Corinthians 14:2)

Gives spiritual discernment

Strengthens us in spiritual warfare

8. The Discipline of Prayer

Prayer is both **a relationship** and **a discipline**. Like any relationship, it requires time, consistency, and intentionality.

a. Set a Time and Place

Jesus often withdrew to pray (Mark 1:35). Find a quiet place and establish a daily rhythm.

b. Use Scripture

Praying the Word of God fuels faith and aligns our prayers with His will.

c. Keep a Journal

Writing down prayers and God's answers strengthens your faith and keeps you focused.

d. Pray with Others

Corporate prayer brings unity and power. Jesus said, "Where two or three gather in My name, there I am with them." (Matthew 18:20)

9. The Power of Fasting and Prayer

Fasting, when combined with prayer, brings spiritual breakthrough. It humbles the flesh and heightens spiritual sensitivity. Isaiah 58 outlines the kind of fast God desires—one that leads to justice, healing, and restoration. Jesus said in Matthew 17:21:
"This kind does not go out except by prayer and fasting."

10. Testimonies and Impact of Prayer

Throughout history, prayer has changed nations, healed bodies, raised the dead, and birthed revivals.

George Müller prayed in food for thousands of orphans without asking anyone but God.

The Welsh Revival began in a prayer meeting.

Countless believers have been saved, healed, and delivered because someone **prayed**.

Prayer is not passive—it is **the most powerful force on earth** when connected to the will of God.

Conclusion: A Call to Prayer

Prayer is not just a practice—it is **your spiritual oxygen**. It is how heaven touches earth. It is how God changes the world—**through you**. Whether you are a seasoned believer or just starting your walk with Christ, the invitation remains the same: *"Call to Me and I will answer you…"* (Jeremiah 33:3)

So pray. Pray when you're strong and when you're weak. Pray when you understand and when you don't. Pray until something breaks—then keep praying. Because prayer is not about moving God closer to us. It's about moving us closer to Him.

The Power of Prayer

Introduction

Prayer is one of the most powerful forces in the universe—not because of the words we say, but because of the God who hears. It is the divine connection point between heaven and earth, between the infinite God and the finite human. Through prayer, miracles are released, hearts are changed, nations are transformed, and lives are renewed.

The power of prayer is not a poetic concept—it is a spiritual reality with eternal consequences. It can alter outcomes, break chains, heal diseases, open doors, and bring revival. It is the oxygen of the Christian life and the secret weapon of every spiritual victory. But what makes prayer powerful? How does it work? And how can believers engage in prayer that changes things? This essay explores the depth and breadth of prayer's power—biblically, historically, and practically.

1. The Foundation of Powerful Prayer

A. What Is Prayer?

Prayer is not a performance or ritual. At its core, prayer is **communion with God**—a relationship built on trust, reverence, and love. It is a two-way interaction: we speak to God, and He responds to us. It includes praise, confession, intercession, thanksgiving, lament, and listening. **Philippians 4:6–7** reminds us: *"Do not be anxious about anything, but in everything by prayer and supplication with thanksgiving let your requests be made known to God. And the peace of God... will guard your hearts and your minds in Christ Jesus."*

Prayer is not about manipulation; it's about alignment. It brings our hearts into agreement with God's will.

B. The Power Lies in the One Who Hears

The power of prayer comes **not from the one praying** but from **the One who answers**. Prayer is powerful because it invokes the **sovereign, omnipotent God**. It places faith not in ourselves, but in Him.

Jeremiah 33:3 declares: *"Call to Me and I will answer you and show you great and mighty things which you do not know."*

When we pray, we tap into the resources of heaven—unlimited wisdom, mercy, grace, and strength.

2. Biblical Evidence of Powerful Prayer

Throughout Scripture, we see example after example of how God moved powerfully through prayer.

A. Moses: Intercessory Prayer Saves a Nation

When Israel sinned with the golden calf (Exodus 32), God planned to destroy them. But Moses interceded:

"Turn from Your fierce wrath... Remember Your servants Abraham, Isaac, and Israel..." (Exodus 32:12–13)

As a result, *"the Lord relented."* Moses' bold intercession saved a nation.

B. Elijah: Prayer That Controls the Weather

Elijah prayed, and it didn't rain for 3.5 years. Then he prayed again, and the heavens opened (James 5:17–18). Elijah's prayer shut and opened the skies.

James uses this to show that **"the prayer of a righteous person is powerful and effective."** (James 5:16)

C. Hannah: Prayer That Births Destiny

Hannah was barren, but she prayed with tears. God heard and gave her Samuel, one of Israel's greatest prophets (1 Samuel 1:10–20).

Her prayer wasn't eloquent—it was **desperate and real**. And it moved heaven.

D. Jesus: Prayer as a Lifestyle

Jesus prayed constantly. He often withdrew to lonely places (Luke

5:16). Before every major decision—calling disciples, performing miracles, going to the cross—Jesus prayed.

Even on the cross, He prayed: "Father, forgive them..." (Luke 23:34)

If the sinless Son of God needed prayer, how much more do we?

3. The Power of Prayer in Church History

A. The Early Church: Built on Prayer

Acts 1:14 says the disciples "joined together constantly in prayer." Acts 2:42 shows the Church devoted to prayer.

Result? Power, growth, and miracles:
Pentecost: 3,000 saved after a prayer meeting (Acts 2)
Peter released from prison by an angel after the Church prayed (Acts 12)
Paul and Silas sang and prayed, and God shook the prison open (Acts 16)

B. Revivals Birthed in Prayer

Most major revivals began in prayer:

The Welsh Revival (1904): Sparked by prayer meetings led by Evan Roberts.

The Moravian Revival (1727): A 100-year prayer chain launched global missions.

Azusa Street Revival (1906): Marked the birth of Pentecostalism through deep, persistent prayer.

C. Heroes of Prayer

George Müller prayed food and funding into orphanages, never asking men.

Reese Howells interceded through WWII, seeing God shift nations.

E.M. Bounds wrote timeless classics on prayer after rising at 4 a.m. to pray daily.

Their lives testify: Prayer **moves history**.

4. Why Prayer Is Powerful Today

A. It Changes Circumstances

Prayer can:

Heal the sick (James 5:14–15)

Restore broken relationships

Provide financial breakthrough
Protect from danger
Guide major decisions
God hears. God acts.

B. It Changes People

You may not always see external change immediately—but prayer always changes the **one who prays**.

It purifies the heart, renews the mind, softens bitterness, and strengthens patience.

2 Corinthians 3:18 says we are transformed "from glory to glory" in God's presence.

C. It Defeats the Enemy

Prayer is spiritual warfare. Paul describes it as part of the **armor of God**:

"And pray in the Spirit on all occasions with all kinds of prayers..." (Ephesians 6:18)
Prayer breaks demonic oppression, cancels the enemy's plans, and releases deliverance.

5. Keys to Powerful Prayer

Not all prayer is equally powerful. Scripture gives us several keys that enhance the effectiveness of our prayers.

A. Pray with Faith

Jesus said:
"Whatever you ask in prayer, believe that you have received it, and it will be yours." (Mark 11:24)
Faith is the currency of heaven. Doubt blocks prayer's power.

B. Pray According to God's Will

1 John 5:14–15:

"If we ask anything according to His will, He hears us..."

We discover God's will through the Bible. The more we know Scripture, the more aligned our prayers become.

C. Pray with a Pure Heart

Psalm 66:18:

"If I had cherished sin in my heart, the Lord would not have listened."

Confession clears the way for powerful prayer.

D. Be Persistent

Luke 18:1–8 tells the story of the persistent widow. Jesus teaches us not to **give up in prayer**.

Breakthrough often comes through perseverance.

6. Different Forms of Powerful Prayer

A. Intercessory Prayer
Standing in the gap for others.
Powerful when motivated by love.
Example: Abraham interceding for Sodom.

B. Prophetic Prayer
Praying with revelation and direction from the Holy Spirit.
Often used in spiritual warfare or healing.
Example: Ezekiel speaking to dry bones.

C. Corporate Prayer
When the Church prays together, power multiplies.
Matthew 18:19–20:
"Where two or three gather in My name, there am I…"

D. Praying in the Spirit

Romans 8:26:
"The Spirit helps us in our weakness... the Spirit himself intercedes for us through wordless groans."
Praying in tongues or spirit-led intercession is a weapon against darkness.

7. How to Develop a Powerful Prayer Life

A. Make It Daily
Set aside time every day. Prayer should be a **rhythm**, not just a reaction.

B. Create a Sacred Space
Find a quiet place. A prayer closet or dedicated corner helps focus your spirit.

C. Use Scripture
Pray God's promises back to Him. The Bible is a prayer guide.
D. Keep a Prayer Journal
Track requests and answers. It builds faith.
E. Fast
Fasting with prayer increases sensitivity and spiritual breakthrough.

8. Obstacles to Powerful Prayer
A. Distraction
Our fast-paced lives pull us away from stillness. Disconnect to reconnect.
B. Discouragement
Unanswered prayer can lead to doubt. Trust God's timing and sovereignty.

C. Pride or Selfish Motives

James 4:3:

"You ask and do not receive, because you ask wrongly, to spend it on your passions."

Check your heart. Is your prayer for God's glory?

9. The Eternal Impact of Prayer

Prayer doesn't end when we say "Amen." It continues to ripple into eternity.

It affects generations (your prayers may shape your grandchildren)

It accumulates in heaven (Revelation 5:8 speaks of the prayers of the saints as incense)

It prepares the way for Christ's return (Matthew 24:14)

No prayer is wasted. Heaven records every cry, every whisper, every tear.

Conclusion: Engage the Power of Prayer

Prayer is not a last resort—it is our first and greatest weapon. It is not the work of the spiritually elite—it is the right and responsibility of every believer. It doesn't require perfection—just a willing heart and a little faith.

Hebrews 4:16 invites us:
"Let us then approach God's throne of grace with confidence, so that we may receive mercy and find grace..."

You are invited. You are heard. You are empowered.
Pray—because God moves when you do.

Holy Spirit: Take Me Home

There is a cry in every human soul—a longing for peace, for purpose, for identity. A yearning not just for a place, but for a Person. This ache is not rooted in emotion alone; it is woven into our spiritual DNA. It's the echo of Eden, the memory of a lost connection with our Creator. When we whisper, "Holy Spirit, take me home," we are expressing the deepest desire of the human heart—to return to where we belong: the presence of God.

The Holy Spirit is the One who leads us home—not just in the eternal sense of heaven, but in the present, as He draws us into communion with the Father through Christ. He is our Comforter, our Counselor, and our Guide. He doesn't just point the way; He walks with us. He carries us.

This essay explores what it means to say "Holy Spirit, take me home," and how the Spirit leads, restores, indwells, and ultimately brings the believer into full fellowship with God.

1. The Longing for Home

The idea of "home" is more than a physical space. It's where you are fully known, deeply loved, and completely safe. For many, "home" on earth is broken—shattered by trauma, rejection, abandonment, or spiritual emptiness. But the longing remains.

Augustine once wrote, *"Our hearts are restless until they rest in You."* This restlessness is a spiritual homesickness. Even if life is good externally, the soul knows when it is distant from its Source.

In Luke 15, Jesus tells the story of the prodigal son—a young man who left his father's house in pursuit of freedom, only to find himself lost, hungry, and alone. But the story turns when he says, *"I will arise and go to my father."* That's the moment the Holy Spirit begins His work in our lives—when we feel the pull to return.

2. The Role of the Holy Spirit

The Holy Spirit is not an abstract force. He is **God Himself**, living in those who believe. He is the one who draws us back to the Father. **John 14:26** says:

"But the Helper, the Holy Spirit, whom the Father will send in My name, He will teach you all things and bring to your remembrance all that I have said to you."

The Spirit:

Convicts us of sin (John 16:8)

Reveals Jesus (John 15:26)

Regenerates us (Titus 3:5)

Guides us into truth (John 16:13)
Seals us for redemption (Ephesians 1:13)
When we pray "Holy Spirit, take me home," we're surrendering to the One who can lead us out of bondage, out of confusion, and into the arms of the Father.

3. Home Is the Presence of God

In the Old Testament, "home" for the Israelites was the **Promised Land**, but even more so, it was the **Presence of God**. The tabernacle and later the temple were places where God dwelled. When the people sinned, the Presence lifted, and they were left empty—even if the physical structures remained.

Now, because of Jesus' sacrifice and resurrection, we don't need a building to experience God. **We are His temple.** The Holy Spirit dwells within us.

1 Corinthians 6:19 —
"Do you not know that your body is a temple of the Holy Spirit within you, whom you have from God?" The presence of the Holy Spirit is the fulfillment of our longing for home. He makes the internal place where we dwell with God—even now. You don't have to wait until heaven to feel at home in Him.

4. The Cry for Restoration

Many people cry, "Holy Spirit, take me home," not from a place of physical lostness but **spiritual**

dryness. Maybe you once walked closely with God but now feel distant. Maybe your worship feels empty, your prayer life weak, or your passion gone. You're not alone.

David, after his sin with Bathsheba, cried out:

"Do not cast me away from Your presence, and do not take Your Holy Spirit from me." (Psalm 51:11) This was the cry of a broken man—but also a man who knew that without the Spirit, he was homeless in the truest sense.

The good news? The Holy Spirit **restores**. He renews, revives, and rebuilds what has been lost. If you feel far from God, know that the Spirit specializes in reconnection.

He can breathe new life into dry bones (Ezekiel 37).

5. The Spirit as a Guide

When Jesus promised the Holy Spirit, He referred to Him as the **Parakletos**—a Greek word meaning Helper, Comforter, or Advocate. The Spirit is not only within you but **beside you**—guiding your steps.
Romans 8:14 says:
"For those who are led by the Spirit of God are the children of God."
When you feel lost in life's decisions or confused by your circumstances, remember: the Holy Spirit is your **spiritual GPS**. He doesn't just drop a map—He walks with you on the journey,

whispering direction, conviction, and encouragement.

Let Him lead. Don't resist His prompts. Whether through Scripture, dreams, peace, or godly counsel, the Spirit knows how to guide you home.

6. The Spirit and Sanctification

Home isn't just a place to go—it's a **way to live**. The Holy Spirit leads us not only into relationship but into **righteousness**. This process is called sanctification—the lifelong transformation that makes us more like Christ.

2 Corinthians 3:18 —
"And we all, who with unveiled faces contemplate the Lord's glory, are being transformed into His

image with ever-increasing glory, which comes from the Lord, who is the Spirit."

As we walk with the Spirit, we begin to:

Desire what God desires

Hate what God hates

Love who God loves

Reflect who God is

This is how the Spirit takes us home—by shaping our character to fit our destination.

7. The Spirit Groans with Us

Sometimes we don't have the words to pray. We're weary, wounded, or just empty. But the Holy Spirit understands. **Romans 8:26** says:

"The Spirit helps us in our weakness... the Spirit himself intercedes for us through wordless groans."

When you say, "Holy Spirit, take me home," even through tears or silence, He hears. He carries your prayer to the Father. He prays what you cannot, and His groan matches yours.

You are never alone. Not even in the darkest place.

8. The Spirit Prepares Us for Heaven

Ultimately, when we cry "take me home," we are also expressing our **eternal hope**. Heaven is not just a destination—it is the full realization of all that God promised. The Holy Spirit is the **guarantee** of that inheritance.

Ephesians 1:13-14 —

"When you believed, you were marked in him with a seal, the promised Holy Spirit... who is a deposit guaranteeing our inheritance."

He prepares us for heaven by:

Convicting us of sin

Keeping us in the faith

Producing the fruit of righteousness

Reminding us of the promises of God

The Spirit is the down payment on your future home—and He ensures you'll make it there.

9. Living with the Spirit Today

You don't have to wait for eternity to walk in the power and presence of the Holy Spirit. He is available **now**.

To walk with the Spirit:

Invite Him daily — Make room for His voice.

Stay in the Word — The Spirit illuminates Scripture.

Obey His leading — He speaks to those who listen.

Pray in the Spirit — Let Him guide your prayers and worship.

Fellowship with believers — The Spirit flows through unity.

10. When You Feel Like Giving Up

There are times when "Holy Spirit, take me home" feels like a **cry of despair**. You're tired. You feel like giving up. Maybe you're even thinking of giving up on life.

Listen carefully: The Holy Spirit is your **life source**, not just your exit strategy. He doesn't just take people *out*—He brings people *through*.

He took Elijah through depression. He took Paul through persecution. He took Jesus through the cross. Whatever you're facing, the Spirit is strong enough to carry you. Don't quit. Home is coming—but until then, the Spirit will sustain you.

Conclusion: Let the Spirit Lead You Home

"Holy Spirit, take me home" is more than a prayer—it's a lifestyle. It's a declaration of trust, a surrender of control, and a yearning for God's presence. It's the voice of a child saying, "Father, I miss You. Lead me back."

And the Spirit answers.

He takes you home:

From sin to salvation

From fear to peace

From wandering to purpose

From religion to relationship

From brokenness to wholeness

From earth to eternity

So wherever you are today— whether far from God or close—let the Holy Spirit take your hand. Let

Him lead you deeper, farther, higher. Let Him bring you home. Because that's where you were always meant to be.

How to Reign with Christ

Introduction

The concept of "reigning with Christ" is one of the most powerful promises found in the Bible. It evokes imagery of authority, victory, rulership, and divine partnership. But it also raises important questions: What does it mean to reign with Christ? Is this reign future, present, or both? And most importantly—**how** do we actually reign with Him in our daily lives?

The promise to reign with Christ is not limited to some distant moment in heaven; it begins **now**, in the heart and life of every believer. It is both **a position** we receive through salvation and **a lifestyle** we grow into through spiritual maturity, obedience, and intimacy with God. This essay will unpack the meaning of reigning with Christ from a biblical perspective, explore its present and future implications, and offer practical steps on how believers can walk in this divine calling.

1. Understanding the Foundation: What It Means to Reign with Christ

a. The Biblical Promise

The idea of reigning with Christ is grounded in Scripture. One of the clearest references is found in **2 Timothy 2:12**:

"If we endure, we will also reign with Him..."

And in **Romans 5:17**:

"For if, by the trespass of the one man, death reigned through that one man, how much more will those who receive God's abundant provision of grace... **reign in life** through the one man, Jesus Christ!"

These passages make it clear: believers are not only saved to be **citizens of heaven** but are also called to be **co-rulers** with Christ, both now and in eternity.

b. Kings and Priests

Revelation 1:6 calls believers **"kings and priests** unto God."** This is an identity, not a metaphor. Christ has redeemed us not only to serve Him but to **reign** with Him, reflecting His authority and executing His will on the earth.

To reign with Christ is to:

Walk in spiritual authority over sin and darkness

Exercise kingdom influence in our calling

Advance God's purposes with power and integrity

Prepare to rule in the coming kingdom with Christ (Revelation 20:6)

2. The Pattern of Christ's Reign

a. Jesus Reigns through Humility and Obedience

Before Jesus wore a crown of glory, He wore a crown of thorns. He reigned not by force but through **humility, obedience, and surrender** to the Father's will. Philippians 2:8-9 says:

"He humbled himself by becoming obedient to death—even death on a cross! Therefore God exalted him to the highest place..."

We cannot reign with Christ without first **walking the path He walked**. Authority in the kingdom is given to those who are willing to humble themselves, serve others, and obey God completely.

b. The Cross Before the Crown

Luke 9:23:

"If anyone wants to come after Me, let him deny himself, take up his cross daily, and follow Me."
This means that to reign with Christ, we must first learn to **die to self**, resist sin, and put God's will above our own desires. Our ruling with Christ begins with **inner victory** over our flesh and submission to His Spirit.

3. Reigning with Christ in the Present

a. Reigning over Sin and Darkness

The first realm in which believers are called to reign is their **own lives**—especially in the area of sin and spiritual bondage.

Romans 6:14:

"For sin shall no longer be your master, because you are not under the law, but under grace."

This means we are not victims—we are **victors**. Through the power of the Holy Spirit, we can say no to sin, defeat temptation, and walk in freedom.

b. Reigning through Identity in Christ

Many Christians fail to reign because they do not know **who they are in Christ**. The enemy attacks through lies and confusion about our spiritual identity.

But Scripture declares:

You are seated with Christ in heavenly places (Ephesians 2:6)

You have access to divine wisdom and power (James 1:5, Acts 1:8)

You are more than a conqueror through Him (Romans 8:37)

To reign with Christ, we must **accept and declare our position** in Him.

c. Reigning through Prayer and Authority

Believers are called to reign by enforcing heaven's will on earth through **prayer, intercession, and spiritual warfare**.

Matthew 16:19:

"I will give you the keys of the kingdom of heaven; whatever you bind on earth will be bound in heaven..."

When we pray with faith and authority, heaven moves. Demons flee. Situations shift. God's power is released.

Reigning with Christ means we **don't beg—we declare**. We pray not from a place of fear, but from our **position in Christ**, as co-heirs and kingdom ambassadors.

4. Reigning with Christ in Relationships and Influence

Reigning with Christ isn't just about private victory—it's also about **public influence**.

a. Kingdom Leadership

Wherever God places you—family, workplace, ministry—you are called to **represent His authority and values**. Reigning doesn't mean controlling others; it means leading by example, serving with love, and standing for righteousness.

Jesus said in Matthew 20:26: "Whoever wants to become great among you must be your servant..." True reign is seen in how we treat people, how we handle pressure, and how we lead with integrity.

b. Reigning in Culture and Society

Daniel, Joseph, and Esther reigned with God's favor in ungodly systems—not by conforming to the world but by standing out in faith. Likewise, believers today must rise up in every sphere—education, business, media, government—and bring kingdom impact.

5. The Cost of Reigning with Christ

a. Endurance and Faithfulness

2 Timothy 2:12:

"If we endure, we will also reign with Him…"

There is no reign without a fight. Reigning with Christ means enduring trials, resisting compromise, and staying faithful when it's hard.

The reward of ruling with Christ is given to the **overcomers** (Revelation 3:21). The race is not to the swift, but to the **steadfast**.

b. Suffering for His Name

Romans 8:17:

"Now if we are children, then we are heirs—heirs of God and co-heirs with Christ, **if indeed we share in his sufferings in order that we may also share in his glory**."

Suffering is not a curse—it's a pathway to glory. Reigning with

Christ involves sharing in His mission, His sacrifice, and sometimes, His rejection.

6. Reigning with Christ in the Future Kingdom

a. The Millennial Reign
Revelation 20:6:
"Blessed and holy are those who share in the first resurrection... they will be priests of God and of Christ and will reign with him for a thousand years."
This refers to the **Millennial Kingdom**, where Christ will physically reign on earth and believers will share in His rule. Faithful believers will be entrusted with **leadership roles**—governing

cities, judging angels, ruling nations
(Luke 19:17, 1 Corinthians 6:3).
Our faithfulness now determines
our authority then.

**b. Eternal Reign in the New
Heaven and Earth**

Revelation 22:5:

"They will reign forever and ever."
Even beyond the Millennial reign,
God's people will reign with Him
for **eternity**—in joy, purpose, and
perfect union with Christ.

Heaven is not a retirement home. It
is an eternal **kingdom assignment**
for those who have proven faithful.

7. How to Prepare to Reign with
Christ

a. Abide in the Word

God's Word is the **training manual** for reigning. The more you know it, the more your authority grows.
Joshua 1:8:
"Keep this Book of the Law always on your lips... Then you will be prosperous and successful."

b. Be Led by the Spirit
Romans 8:14:
"For those who are led by the Spirit of God are the children of God."
Authority comes from intimacy. Spend time daily with the Holy Spirit. Let Him refine your character and direct your steps.

c. Stay Humble and Teachable
Pride destroys kings; humility preserves them.
James 4:10:
"Humble yourselves before the Lord, and He will lift you up."

A teachable spirit is one that can be entrusted with much.

d. Commit to the Local Church

God's kingdom operates through **community**. Serving in the body of Christ is both preparation and practice for reigning.

Hebrews 10:25 reminds us not to forsake gathering together. Your faith grows when you walk with others.

Conclusion

To reign with Christ is not just a future reward—it's a present **calling**. It's a divine invitation to walk in spiritual authority, live in holiness, and represent heaven on earth.

Christ has already won the victory. He invites us not only to share in the spoils, but to share in the **mission**, the **burden**, and the **glory**.

So how do we reign with Christ? We **surrender**, we **serve**, we **walk in the Spirit**, and we **stand firm** in truth. We fight the good fight of faith, not as orphans, but as **sons and daughters of the King**. And one day soon, when He returns in glory, we will reign with Him— forever.

The Power of Resurrection

The resurrection of Jesus Christ is the cornerstone of the Christian faith. It is more than an event recorded in history—it is a living, active reality that continues to transform lives today. The **power of resurrection** is not confined to what happened in the tomb over two thousand years ago. Instead, it is a supernatural force that brings dead things to life—spiritually, emotionally, relationally, and even physically. It defines the Christian's identity, empowers their purpose, and secures their eternal hope. The Apostle Paul declared in **Philippians 3:10**, *"I want to know Christ—yes, to know the power of his resurrection and participation in his sufferings, becoming like him in his death."* This statement encapsulates a deep truth: the resurrection isn't just a belief—it's a power to be experienced.

In this comprehensive study, we will explore what the resurrection is, what kind of power it holds, how it affects the believer's life, and how we can live in that power today.

1. Understanding the Resurrection

The Historical Event

The resurrection of Jesus Christ refers to His rising from the dead on the third day after His crucifixion. It is recorded in all four Gospels (Matthew 28, Mark 16, Luke 24, John 20), and confirmed throughout the New Testament. It validated Jesus' divine identity and fulfilled the Scriptures that foretold a Messiah who would conquer death.

Without the resurrection, Christianity would have no foundation. Paul emphasizes in **1 Corinthians 15:17**, *"If Christ has not been raised, your faith is futile; you are still in your sins."* The resurrection proves that:

Jesus is the Son of God (Romans 1:4)

Death and sin have been conquered (1 Corinthians 15:54-57)

Believers will also be raised to eternal life (1 Thessalonians 4:14)

2. What Is the Power of Resurrection?

The **power of resurrection** is the **life-giving, death-defeating, sin-breaking, hope-restoring power of God**. It is the force that raised Jesus from the dead, and it is still active and accessible to believers today.

The Greek Word: *Dunamis*
In the New Testament, the word for "power" used in connection with the resurrection is **dunamis**—from which we get the English word "dynamite." It speaks of **explosive, miraculous strength and ability**.

Romans 8:11 says,
"And if the Spirit of him who raised Jesus from the dead is living in you, he who raised Christ from the dead will also give life to your mortal

bodies through his Spirit, who lives in you."

This means resurrection power is **not abstract**—it is personal. The very same Spirit that raised Christ lives in every believer. That power is available to transform, heal, and sustain them daily.

3. Resurrection Power Over Sin and Death

The most obvious expression of resurrection power is in **overcoming death**. But it also breaks the grip of sin.

Romans 6:4-5 says:

"We were therefore buried with him through baptism into death in order that, just as Christ was raised

from the dead... we too may live a new life."
Through resurrection power:
Sin's penalty is paid.
Sin's power is broken.
Sin's presence will one day be removed.
Believers are no longer **slaves to sin** but can now **walk in righteousness** because resurrection power has changed their spiritual DNA. They are no longer bound by the nature of Adam but reborn through Christ.

4. Resurrection Power Gives New Life

The resurrection brings more than freedom from sin—it brings

newness of life. This new life involves a transformation of:

Mind: Renewed by the truth (Romans 12:2)

Heart: Filled with love and compassion (Ezekiel 36:26)

Purpose: Called to glorify God and serve others (Ephesians 2:10)

2 Corinthians 5:17 declares: "If anyone is in Christ, the new creation has come: The old has gone, the new is here!" Resurrection power takes what was dead—dreams, hope, identity—and brings it back to life. It renews a broken heart, a weary soul, or a failing marriage. Just as Jesus called Lazarus from the grave, He still speaks life over situations that seem hopeless.

5. Resurrection Power Gives Victory Over the Enemy

Jesus' resurrection is a **public defeat** of Satan's kingdom. **Colossians 2:15** says,
"And having disarmed the powers and authorities, he made a public spectacle of them, triumphing over them by the cross."
The resurrection confirms that the enemy has:
No legal authority over believers
No final say over their destiny
No power to separate them from God's love
Through resurrection power, Christians are not fighting for victory—they are fighting **from**

victory. Spiritual warfare is real, but believers overcome "by the blood of the Lamb and the word of their testimony" (Revelation 12:11), because the resurrection sealed the final outcome.

6. Resurrection Power for Daily Living

Resurrection power isn't just for heaven—it's for **daily life on earth**. It strengthens believers to:
Endure trials with joy
Love unconditionally
Forgive enemies
Live holy in a corrupt world
Resist temptation
Serve sacrificially

Paul writes in **Ephesians 1:19-20** about the "incomparably great power for us who believe," which is the **same power** that raised Christ from the dead.

That means resurrection power:
Helps you rise above depression, shame, and fear.
Empowers you to be bold when you feel weak.
Enables you to trust when life doesn't make sense.

7. Resurrection Power Gives Eternal Hope

Beyond this life, resurrection power secures our **eternal future**. The same Spirit who raised Jesus will also raise every believer.

1 Corinthians 15:52-54 tells us that at Christ's return,
"the dead will be raised imperishable, and we will be changed... then the saying that is written will come true: 'Death has been swallowed up in victory.'"
The resurrection guarantees:
Physical resurrection of the body
Eternal life with God
No more death, sorrow, or pain
(Revelation 21:4)
This is the Christian's **blessed hope**—not just escaping hell, but living in fullness and glory with Jesus forever.

8. How to Live in Resurrection Power

Many believers understand resurrection as a doctrine but have not **experienced its power**. Here are ways to walk in that power daily:

A. Believe the Gospel Deeply

The resurrection is not just a symbol—it is the **core** of the gospel. Believe it, trust it, and confess it regularly.

Romans 10:9 says:

"If you declare with your mouth, 'Jesus is Lord,' and believe in your heart that God raised him from the dead, you will be saved."

B. Be Filled With the Holy Spirit

The Holy Spirit is the one who applies resurrection power in your life. Ask to be filled, led, and empowered daily.

Acts 1:8 — *"You will receive power when the Holy Spirit comes upon you..."*

C. Abide in Christ

Stay connected to the source of life. Jesus said in **John 15:5**,

"Apart from me, you can do nothing."

Through prayer, Scripture, and obedience, the power of resurrection flows into every area of your life.

D. Speak Resurrection Truth

Life and death are in the power of the tongue (Proverbs 18:21). Speak God's promises over your circumstances. Don't agree with death, fear, or defeat—declare what God says.

E. Live With Boldness and Faith
The early church preached boldly because they believed in the resurrection. Let your life be a testimony. Share the gospel, love radically, and live with heavenly courage.

9. Resurrection Power in the Church

The resurrection is not just for individuals—it is the **foundation of the Church**. A resurrection-powered church is marked by:
Unity and **love**
Miracles, **healing**, and **deliverance**
Bold preaching
Hope in suffering

Radical generosity
Sadly, many churches operate with form but lack power. Paul warned of people *"having a form of godliness but denying its power"* (2 Timothy 3:5). True revival comes when the Church rediscovers and walks in resurrection power.

10. The Resurrection and the End Times

The resurrection is also tied to the **second coming of Christ**. The final resurrection will occur when Jesus returns, and all the dead in Christ will rise.
1 Thessalonians 4:16-17:

"For the Lord himself will come down from heaven... and the dead in Christ will rise first."
Believers will be changed in the twinkling of an eye, clothed in immortality, and ushered into eternal glory. This truth should fuel hope and perseverance, especially in the last days.

Conclusion: Living in the Power of Resurrection

The **power of resurrection** is not confined to Easter Sunday or theological textbooks. It is a living reality, available every day to those who believe. It breaks chains, restores hope, transforms lives, and gives eternal victory.

If you are in Christ, resurrection power is in you.
You are not defeated—you are raised. You are not bound—you are free. You are not dead—you are alive.
Let the power that raised Jesus from the dead raise you too— today and forever.

Spiritual warfare is an important concept within Christianity that highlights the continual conflict between good and evil spiritual forces. This idea recognizes that believers are part of a genuine, albeit unseen, struggle that goes beyond the physical world, impacting their daily lives, choices, and futures. For those

aiming to lead a victorious Christian life, grasping the concept of spiritual warfare is vital as it unveils enemy strategies and provides believers with the necessary tools to prevail.

Biblical Foundation of Spiritual Warfare

The scriptural basis for spiritual warfare can be found in various Bible passages, notably Ephesians 6:10-18. In this passage, the Apostle Paul encourages believers to "put on the full armor of God" to withstand the devil's schemes. He clarifies that "our struggle is not against flesh and blood, but against the rulers, authorities, powers of this dark world, and the spiritual forces of evil in heavenly realms." This clearly indicates that spiritual warfare is not merely figurative but an actual reality. The Bible depicts Satan as a true adversary, a deceiver intent on opposing God and harming His followers. Nonetheless, it also asserts that through His death and resurrection, Jesus has already conquered Satan, meaning believers engage in the fight from a position of victory rather than striving for it.

Tactics of the Enemy

Comprehending the enemy's tactics is essential in spiritual warfare. Often, the devil's attacks are subtle rather than blatant. He typically employs deception, temptation, and accusation to weaken believers' faith and disrupt their connection with God.

- **Deception**: Referred to as "the father of lies" (John 8:44), Satan twists the truth, generates confusion, and sows doubt about God's word. His deception of Eve in the Garden of Eden exemplifies this manipulation.

- **Temptation**: The devil entices believers to sin, diverting them from God's will by appealing to their pride, greed, lust, and other sinful desires, as he did with Jesus in the wilderness.

- **Accusation**: Described in Revelation 12:10 as "the accuser of our brothers and sisters," Satan attempts to condemn believers and convince them they are unworthy of God's love and forgiveness.

Thus, spiritual warfare is not only about overt confrontations with evil; it often plays out in more subtle, psychological forms within our thoughts, emotions, and choices.

The Armor of God

In Ephesians 6, Paul describes the spiritual armor available to believers. Each component symbolizes a crucial aspect of defense and offense in spiritual warfare.

- **Belt of Truth**: Truth is foundational, safeguarding against deception and securing all other armor pieces.

- **Breastplate of Righteousness**: Righteousness protects the heart. A right standing with God shields believers from guilt and shame.

- **Feet Fitted with the Gospel of Peace**: The stability provided by the gospel enables believers to remain steadfast amid turmoil.

- **Shield of Faith**: Faith serves to extinguish the fiery arrows of doubt, fear, and falsehoods by trusting in God's promises regardless of circumstances.

- **Helmet of Salvation**: Salvation protects the mind, assuring believers of their security in Christ against mental assaults.

- **Sword of the Spirit**: The Word of God is the sole offensive weapon, powerful enough to counter the enemy, as exemplified by Jesus during His temptation.

- **Prayer**: Although not labelled as a piece of armor, Paul emphasizes the importance of prayer as a means for believers to connect with God and access divine strength.

The Battlefield of the Mind

One of the most significant arenas in spiritual warfare is the mind. Paul reminds believers in 2 Corinthians 10:3-5 that they possess divine authority "to demolish strongholds" which are arguments and pretensions opposing God's knowledge. He encourages them to "take captive every thought to make it obedient to Christ." This mental battle often entails resisting lies about identity, worth, and God's character. Many believers face fears, anxieties, depression, or shame—struggles that the enemy can exploit. Therefore, renewing the mind with Scripture, prayer, and supportive spiritual communities is crucial for achieving victory.

The Power of the Cross

The encouraging aspect of spiritual warfare is that the outcome has already been determined. Jesus Christ overcame darkness through His death and resurrection. Colossians 2:15 declares, "And having disarmed the powers and authorities, he made a public spectacle of them, triumphing over them by the cross." Consequently, believers fight not for victory but from a place of victory, possessing the authority to resist the devil as instructed in James 4:7: "Submit yourselves, then, to God. Resist the devil, and he will flee from you." While believers are not immune to attacks, they are not powerless. By remaining in Christ, adhering to His Word, and donning the provided spiritual armor, they can triumph.

The Importance of Community and Worship

Spiritual warfare is not meant to be faced alone. God intended for believers to live and engage in battle within a community. Isolation leaves individuals vulnerable, whereas fellowship offers strength, encouragement, and accountability. Worship serves as a potent weapon, redirecting focus from challenges to God, drawing His presence, and disorienting the enemy. For instance, when Paul and Silas worshiped in prison in Acts 16, a miraculous earthquake led to their release— a breakthrough brought about through praise.

Identifying Signs of Spiritual Attack

Being able to recognize signs of spiritual warfare is crucial for appropriate responses. These may include:

- Ongoing temptation or feelings of discouragement

- Confusion or difficulty in concentrating spiritually

- Unusual conflicts in relationships

- Heightened fear or anxiety

- A sense of distance from God, despite efforts to engage with Him

These signs may not always indicate spiritual warfare individually, but when they occur together, especially during periods of spiritual growth or ministry, they may signal an attack.

How to Respond

- **Stand on the Word**: Counter lies and temptations with Scripture.

- **Pray with Authority**: Pray assertively, not from fear, but with the authority given by Christ.

- **Seek Support**: Share challenges with trusted believers

who can provide prayer and support.

- **Remain Obedient**: Continue to obey God, even when faced with difficulties, as faithfulness itself is a form of warfare.

- **Worship Intentionally**: Praise God, even in hardship, as it changes the atmosphere and perspective.

Conclusion

Spiritual warfare is a reality every Christian will confront, yet it is not a battle to dread. God has equipped His followers with everything necessary to stand firm and overcome. The focus should not be on personal strength but on staying connected to Jesus, relying on His truth, and moving in the power of the Holy Spirit. Victory in spiritual warfare hinges not on dramatic actions, but on daily faithfulness—trusting God's promises, resisting the enemy's lies, and glowing as lights in darkness. As believers remain vigilant, equipped, and surrendered to God, they can walk in the victory that Christ has already secured.

When we walk in the Spirit, we become more like Christ—not by trying harder, but by surrendering more deeply. The fruit of the Spirit becomes evident in our lives, and we experience the freedom, peace, and joy that come from walking in step with our Creator.

Ultimately, walking in the Spirit glorifies God and brings blessing not only to us but to everyone around us. It's the kind of life we were created to live—a life marked by love, guided by truth, and empowered by grace.

How to Overcome the Power of Darkness

The power of darkness is a term used in the Bible to describe the influence and work of evil in the world—led by Satan and his demonic forces. It represents the realm of sin, deception, fear, bondage, and spiritual death. Every person, whether aware or not, is affected by this darkness in some way. But Scripture teaches that through Christ, we are not only delivered from darkness but empowered to overcome it. Overcoming the power of darkness is not a passive process; it is an intentional and active spiritual battle that involves faith, knowledge of the truth, and reliance on God.

Understanding the Power of Darkness

Before learning how to overcome darkness, it's important to understand what it is. Darkness in the spiritual sense is more than the absence of physical light—it is the absence of God's presence and truth. It is a domain where sin reigns, where lies are believed, where fear dominates, and where spiritual blindness prevails. Colossians 1:13 says, "He has delivered us from the power of darkness and conveyed us into the kingdom of the Son of His love." This verse emphasizes that the power of darkness is real, but it also makes clear that Christ has rescued believers from it. Still, believers must learn how to walk in the light and resist being pulled back into old patterns and lies. The power of darkness often manifests through:

Temptation to sin

Bondage to destructive habits

Oppression through fear, depression, or anxiety

Confusion, doubt, or deception

Relational conflict and division

Spiritual apathy or resistance to God

While darkness may seem powerful, it cannot stand against the light of God. Overcoming it starts with recognizing its influence and replacing it with God's truth and presence.

1. Accept Jesus Christ as Lord and Savior

The most crucial step in overcoming the power of darkness is surrendering your life to Jesus Christ. Without Christ, no person has the strength or authority to defeat spiritual darkness. John 8:12 records Jesus saying, "I am the light of the world. Whoever follows me will never walk in darkness but will have the light of life."

Jesus broke the power of darkness when He died on the cross and rose again. His resurrection proved His victory over sin, death, and Satan. By putting your faith in Christ, you are transferred from the kingdom of darkness into the kingdom of light.

Salvation is not just about going to heaven one day—it's about living in spiritual freedom now. Through

Jesus, you are given authority over darkness, and the Holy Spirit comes to live within you, guiding you into truth and power.

2. Fill Your Life with God's Word

The Word of God is described as a light that dispels darkness. Psalm 119:105 says, "Your word is a lamp to my feet and a light to my path." Darkness thrives in ignorance and confusion, but truth brings clarity and freedom.

To overcome darkness, you must know what God says. Regular Bible reading, study, and meditation help renew your mind and expose the lies that darkness uses to hold you captive.

When Jesus was tempted by Satan in the wilderness, He responded with Scripture each time. The Word of God is a weapon against the enemy. Knowing it equips you to recognize deception and walk in spiritual authority.

3. Pray with Authority

Prayer is not only communication with God—it's a means of spiritual warfare. In Ephesians 6, Paul describes prayer as essential to putting on the full armor of God. He says to "pray in the Spirit on all occasions with all kinds of prayers and requests."

Through prayer, you invite God's power into your circumstances, declare His promises, and resist the enemy's influence. James 4:7 says, "Submit yourselves, then, to God. Resist the devil, and he will flee from you." Prayer is how you do both.

You don't need elaborate words—
just sincere, faith-filled prayers.
Pray over your mind, your home,
your family, and your relationships.
Ask for the Holy Spirit's help and
for the light of God's presence to
shine in every area of your life.

4. Break Agreement with Darkness

Many people unknowingly partner
with darkness by agreeing with lies,
holding onto unforgiveness,
participating in sinful behaviors, or
entertaining demonic influences.
To overcome darkness, you must
renounce those agreements.
This may involve confessing sin,
repenting of ungodly beliefs, and
letting go of anything that opposes
God's truth. For example, if you
believe you are worthless or

unloved, you are agreeing with darkness. God's truth says you are fearfully and wonderfully made and deeply loved by Him.

Ask the Holy Spirit to reveal areas where darkness has had a foothold in your life. Then, break those strongholds through confession, repentance, and declaration of the truth.

5. Cultivate a Life of Worship

Worship is a powerful weapon against darkness. It shifts your focus from fear to faith, from lies to truth, and from despair to hope. In worship, God's presence becomes tangible, and where His presence is, darkness cannot stay.

Acts 16 tells of Paul and Silas worshiping in prison. As they sang, an earthquake shook the foundations, their chains fell off, and the doors opened. Worship invites breakthrough.

Make worship a regular part of your life—not just in church, but privately. Sing, pray, praise, and express love for God. Let worship be your response even in hardship, and you will see darkness flee.

6. Stay in Community

Isolation is one of darkness's greatest tools. When people are isolated, they become vulnerable to lies, discouragement, and spiritual attack. God designed believers to live in community.

Surround yourself with other believers who encourage your faith, pray with you, and hold you accountable. Share your struggles and victories. Let others help carry your burdens and speak truth when you forget it.

Hebrews 10:25 reminds believers not to neglect meeting together, especially as the day of Christ's return draws near. There is strength in unity, and light shines brighter when it's shared.

7. Walk in the Light Daily

Overcoming darkness isn't a one-time event—it's a daily choice to walk in the light. This means living with integrity, pursuing holiness, and staying close to God.

1 John 1:7 says, "But if we walk in the light, as he is in the light, we have fellowship with one another, and the blood of Jesus...purifies us from all sin." Walking in the light includes being honest, confessing

sin, and living openly before God and others.

It also means guarding your heart and mind. Be cautious about what you watch, listen to, and allow into your life. Feed your spirit with things that strengthen you, not weaken you.

Conclusion

The power of darkness is real, but it is no match for the light of Christ. Through Jesus, you have everything you need to overcome. You don't have to live in fear, confusion, or bondage. You can live in freedom, peace, and victory.

Overcoming darkness requires commitment, faith, and spiritual discipline. It involves knowing who you are in Christ, using the Word as your weapon, and walking daily in

God's truth. As you do, the grip of darkness will loosen, and the light of God will shine more brightly in and through your life.

How to Move Closer to God

In a world filled with distractions, uncertainties, and spiritual dryness, many people find themselves asking, "How can I move closer to God?" Whether you've known God for years or are just beginning your spiritual journey, the longing to grow closer to Him is a sign of a heart that desires more than the surface level of faith. Drawing near to God is not about religious rituals or earning His love—it's about developing a deep, authentic relationship with the One who created you.

James 4:8 says, "Draw near to God, and He will draw near to you." This promise assures us that when we take steps toward God, He meets us where we are. Moving closer to Him is both a process and a lifestyle that involves intentionality, humility, and transformation.

1. Develop a Personal Relationship with Jesus

The foundation of closeness to God begins with a relationship with Jesus Christ. Jesus said in John 14:6, "I am the way and the truth and the life. No one comes to the Father except through me." Without Jesus, it's impossible to truly know God because He is the bridge between humanity and the divine.

Accepting Jesus as Lord and Savior is the first step in drawing near. This involves repentance—turning away from sin—and faith, believing that Jesus died and rose again to forgive your sins and give you eternal life. Salvation is not about being "good enough" but about receiving God's grace.

Once you've entered into a relationship with Jesus, you can begin growing closer to God through everyday choices and spiritual practices.

2. Make Time for Prayer

Prayer is the lifeline of your relationship with God. Just like any friendship or connection, communication is essential. Prayer is more than presenting a list of needs; it's an ongoing conversation with your Heavenly Father.

You can talk to God about anything—your fears, your joys, your doubts, your decisions. When you pray, you invite Him into every part of your life. Philippians 4:6 encourages believers, "Do not be anxious about anything, but in everything by prayer and supplication with thanksgiving let your requests be made known to God."

Make prayer a daily habit. Find a quiet place, eliminate distractions, and pour out your heart. Listen, too—God speaks, often through gentle nudges or Scripture.

3. Read and Meditate on the Bible

The Bible is God's voice in written form. If you want to get to know Him more intimately, His Word is where He reveals His character, promises, and plans. Psalm 119:105 says, "Your word is a lamp to my feet and a light to my path." Through the Bible, you learn who God is and how He wants you to live.

Reading Scripture daily, even if it's just a few verses, builds your spiritual foundation. Go beyond reading—meditate on what you read. Ask, "What does this teach me about God? How can I apply this to my life?"

There are many Bible reading plans to help guide you, from beginner-friendly devotionals to in-depth studies. The more you immerse yourself in the Word, the more you'll recognize God's voice and direction.

4. Worship from the Heart

Worship is a powerful way to move closer to God. It's not confined to singing in church—it's a lifestyle of honoring and glorifying Him in everything you do. Romans 12:1 urges believers to "offer your bodies as a living sacrifice, holy and pleasing to God—this is your true and proper worship."

When you sing, pray, or reflect on God's goodness, you express love and reverence. Worship shifts your focus from yourself to the greatness of God. It aligns your heart with His and strengthens your connection to Him.

Make time to worship alone and with others. Play worship music, sing from your heart, and express gratitude. Even in tough times, worship brings you into God's presence and helps you sense His closeness.

5. Obey God's Word

Obedience is a key step in growing closer to God. Jesus said in John 14:23, "Anyone who loves me will obey my teaching. My Father will love them, and we will come to them and make our home with them." Obedience is not about following rules for the sake of religion; it's a response of love and trust.

As you read Scripture, you'll encounter areas of your life that need change—attitudes, habits, relationships. Choosing to obey, even when it's hard or inconvenient, deepens your intimacy with God. It demonstrates that you value His will more than your own.

Obedience also builds spiritual maturity. When you trust God enough to follow His lead, you grow stronger in faith and experience more of His presence and guidance.

6. Confess and Repent Regularly

Sin creates distance between you and God. While salvation covers your sin once and for all, unconfessed sin can hinder your fellowship with Him. That's why ongoing confession and repentance are vital.

1 John 1:9 promises, "If we confess our sins, he is faithful and just to

forgive us and cleanse us from all unrighteousness." Regularly examine your heart. Be honest about your struggles, failures, and temptations. Ask God to forgive you and help you walk in holiness. Repentance is not just saying "sorry"—it's turning away from sin and turning back to God. When you repent, you remove barriers and restore the closeness that sin tries to steal.

7. Get Involved in a Faith Community

God never meant for you to walk your spiritual journey alone. Being part of a community of believers provides encouragement, accountability, and shared wisdom. Hebrews 10:24-25 says, "Let us consider how we may spur one another on toward love and good deeds...not giving up meeting together...but encouraging one another."

Attend church regularly, join a Bible study group, or find a mentor. Surrounding yourself with others who are seeking God will strengthen your own faith and help you grow.

In community, you also have opportunities to serve others, use your spiritual gifts, and reflect God's love in practical ways—all of which draw you closer to His heart.

8. Practice Gratitude and Trust

Moving closer to God involves learning to trust Him, even when life is uncertain or painful. Gratitude helps you shift your perspective from problems to blessings, and trust anchors you in God's character.

Proverbs 3:5-6 says, "Trust in the Lord with all your heart and lean not on your own understanding; in all your ways submit to him, and he will make your paths straight." The more you trust God with your future, your relationships, and your fears, the more you'll experience His peace and presence.

Keep a gratitude journal. Reflect on what God has done in your life. When you face difficulties, remember past victories. Trust that God is working, even when you can't see it.

9. Seek the Holy Spirit's Guidance

The Holy Spirit is God's presence living in you. He teaches, comforts, convicts, and empowers you to live for Christ. Building a relationship with the Holy Spirit will deepen your connection to God.

Ask the Holy Spirit to fill you daily, to guide your decisions, and to produce spiritual fruit in your life. Listen for His voice and be sensitive to His prompting. As you walk in the Spirit, you'll find yourself growing closer to God in ways you never imagined.

Conclusion

Moving closer to God is not a formula—it's a relationship. It's cultivated over time through prayer, Scripture, worship, obedience, and community. It involves letting go of sin, embracing grace, and trusting in God's love every day.

The journey is personal, but the invitation is universal: God desires to be close to you. As you take steps toward Him, He promises to meet you with open arms, guiding you deeper into His presence, peace, and purpose.

The Spirit-Filled Man
A "Spirit-filled man" is a person whose life is deeply influenced, empowered, and guided by the Holy Spirit. This concept is central to Christian faith and discipleship. The Bible teaches that when a person accepts Jesus Christ as Lord and Savior, they receive the indwelling of the Holy Spirit.

However, being filled with the Spirit goes beyond simple indwelling—it refers to a continuous state of being led, transformed, and empowered by the presence of God.

In a world filled with self-reliance, pride, and worldly ambition, the Spirit-filled man stands out. His life reflects the character of Christ, not because of personal strength or effort, but because the Spirit of God is active within him. Understanding who the Spirit-filled man is and how he lives can challenge and inspire every believer to pursue a deeper, more meaningful walk with God.

1. Understanding the Holy Spirit's Role

To grasp what it means to be a Spirit-filled man, one must first understand the role of the Holy Spirit. The Holy Spirit is the third person of the Trinity—equal with the Father and the Son. Jesus promised His followers that He would send the Holy Spirit to be their Comforter, Teacher, and Guide (John 14:16-17, 26).

The Spirit brings conviction of sin, reveals truth, empowers for service, and produces godly character. The Spirit-filled man does not live by his own power or wisdom. Instead, he yields to the Spirit, depending on God for strength, direction, and growth.

Paul writes in **Ephesians 5:18**, "Do not get drunk on wine, which leads to debauchery. Instead, be filled with the Spirit." The comparison here is striking. Just as alcohol influences behavior and emotions, the Spirit should be the controlling influence in a believer's life. The verb "be filled" is in the present tense, indicating an ongoing process, not a one-time event.

2. The Fruit of the Spirit

One of the clearest signs of a Spirit-filled life is the manifestation of the **fruit of the Spirit**, as outlined in **Galatians 5:22-23**: "But the fruit of the Spirit is love, joy, peace, forbearance (patience), kindness, goodness, faithfulness, gentleness and self-control."

These virtues are not produced through human effort, but through the Holy Spirit's work in a surrendered heart. A Spirit-filled man exhibits love, even when it's hard. He maintains joy, even in trials. He pursues peace, chooses patience, practices kindness, and remains faithful, even when others don't. These traits grow as he walks with God daily.

This fruit is not about external behavior alone—it reveals the transformation taking place within. The Spirit-filled man is not perfect, but he is growing. His life is marked by grace, humility, and an increasing resemblance to Jesus Christ.

3. Empowered for Service

A Spirit-filled man is not only inwardly transformed; he is outwardly empowered to serve. In the early church, the outpouring of the Holy Spirit enabled believers to boldly proclaim the gospel, heal the sick, cast out demons, and live out their calling despite persecution.

Acts 1:8 records Jesus' words: "But you will receive power when the Holy Spirit comes on you; and you will be my witnesses..." This power is not for personal glory, but for effective ministry and mission.

Each believer is given spiritual gifts by the Spirit (1 Corinthians 12). These may include teaching, prophecy, encouragement, leadership, mercy, and others. The Spirit-filled man recognizes and uses his gifts to serve the Church and reach the lost. His life is not centered on self, but on advancing the kingdom of God.

4. A Life of Surrender and Obedience

To be filled with the Spirit requires continual **surrender**. The Spirit-filled man does not cling to his own agenda but yields daily to God's will. Romans 12:1 calls believers to offer themselves as "living sacrifices, holy and pleasing to God."

This surrender is not passive—it's active and intentional. It means saying "yes" to God's promptings and "no" to the flesh. It means choosing forgiveness over bitterness, purity over compromise, humility over pride.

Obedience is not always easy, but it is the pathway to deeper intimacy with God. The Spirit-filled man doesn't obey out of fear, but out of love. He trusts that God's ways are higher and that true life is found in submission to Him.

5. A Man of Prayer and the Word

The Spirit-filled man prioritizes communion with God through **prayer** and the **Word of God**. Prayer is more than a ritual—it is the heartbeat of his relationship with God. In prayer, he worships, listens, intercedes, and finds strength.

The Word is his spiritual nourishment. Through Scripture, he learns God's character, discerns truth, and renews his mind. Ephesians 6 calls the Word of God "the sword of the Spirit," a vital weapon in spiritual warfare.

By remaining rooted in prayer and Scripture, the Spirit-filled man stays aligned with God's will and resists the lies of the enemy.

6. Walking in Humility and Dependence

A true mark of a Spirit-filled life is **humility**. The more a man walks with the Spirit, the more he recognizes his need for God. He does not boast in his achievements or rely on his own strength. He understands that every good thing in his life is a gift from above. Jesus, though equal with God, humbled Himself and served others (Philippians 2:5-8). The Spirit-filled man follows this example. He leads by serving. He listens before speaking. He gives rather than grasps.

His dependence on God is not a weakness—it is his greatest strength. In his weakness, God's power is made perfect (2 Corinthians 12:9).

7. A Witness to the World

Finally, the Spirit-filled man lives as a **witness** to a watching world. His life tells the story of redemption, transformation, and hope. People are drawn not just to his words, but to his character and peace.

He is bold in sharing the gospel, but he does so with compassion and respect. He stands for truth, but speaks it in love. His life points others to Christ, not himself.

In a world desperate for authenticity and hope, the Spirit-filled man is a beacon of light. He reflects Jesus in everyday life—at home, at work, and in the community.

Conclusion

The Spirit-filled man is not a spiritual elite or a flawless saint. He is an ordinary person made extraordinary by the presence of the Holy Spirit. His life is one of surrender, growth, service, and love.

To become a Spirit-filled man, one must cultivate a heart that is open, humble, and hungry for God. It is not about striving harder, but about yielding deeper. As the Holy Spirit fills and leads, every aspect of a man's life is transformed—his thoughts, actions, relationships, and purpose.

Ultimately, the Spirit-filled man is one who lives not for himself, but for the glory of God. And in doing so, he experiences the fullness of life that Jesus promised.

How to Be Directed by the Holy Spirit

One of the greatest privileges of the Christian life is being guided by the Holy Spirit. God never intended for His people to navigate life alone. From the moment a person is saved, the Holy Spirit comes to dwell within them—not just as a silent presence, but as an active guide, teacher, and comforter. Yet many believers still ask: **"How can I be directed by the Holy Spirit?"** Being directed by the Holy Spirit means living in constant awareness of His presence, listening for His voice, and allowing Him to influence your decisions, actions, and attitudes. It requires humility, obedience, and spiritual sensitivity. This divine guidance doesn't always come through dramatic revelations—it often comes through gentle promptings, Scripture, prayer, and inner conviction.

1. Receive the Holy Spirit Through Faith in Christ

Before a person can be led by the Holy Spirit, they must be **born again** through faith in Jesus Christ. According to Romans 8:9, "If anyone does not have the Spirit of Christ, they do not belong to Christ." The first step in being directed by the Holy Spirit is to **invite Jesus into your heart as Lord and Savior**.

When you give your life to Christ, you receive the Holy Spirit as a gift

(Acts 2:38). He becomes your constant companion, working within you to transform your heart and guide your steps.

2. Develop a Personal Relationship With the Holy Spirit

The Holy Spirit is not an abstract force—He is a **person**. He has emotions, will, and intellect. To be directed by Him, you must grow in relationship with Him. Just like any friendship, this relationship deepens through time, attention, and intentional communication. Speak to the Holy Spirit daily. Ask Him to lead you, teach you, and fill you. Acknowledge His presence in your life. When you treat Him as a real and present guide, you become more attuned to His leading.

2 Corinthians 13:14 refers to "the fellowship of the Holy Spirit." This fellowship is not reserved for super-spiritual people—it's for every believer who desires to walk closely with God.

3. Spend Time in the Word of God

One of the primary ways the Holy Spirit directs believers is through **Scripture**. He inspired the Word, and He uses it to guide, correct, and teach us (2 Timothy 3:16-17). When you read the Bible, the Holy Spirit illuminates truth and brings personal application to your life. Psalm 119:105 says, "Your word is a lamp to my feet and a light to my path." If you want to be directed by the Spirit, immerse yourself in the Word. The more Scripture you know, the more clearly you will hear God's voice.

Many times, guidance from the Holy Spirit comes in the form of a verse that suddenly speaks directly to your situation. As you meditate on Scripture, your mind is renewed, and your heart is aligned with God's will.

4. Cultivate a Sensitive and Obedient Heart

To be led by the Holy Spirit, you must have a heart that is **sensitive** to His promptings and **quick to obey**. The Spirit often speaks through inner nudges, convictions, or peace—or lack thereof.

Romans 8:14 says, "For those who are led by the Spirit of God are the children of God." This guidance is personal and continuous. However, if you ignore His leading or resist His correction, your spiritual sensitivity can diminish.

Ask God to soften your heart and give you the courage to obey—even when it's difficult. When the Spirit nudges you to speak to someone, change your plans, confess a sin, or step out in faith, respond with willingness. The more you obey, the more clearly you'll hear His voice.

5. Pray and Wait for His Guidance

Prayer is how we align our hearts with God and listen for the Holy Spirit's direction. Philippians 4:6-7 teaches us to present our requests to God and that His peace will guard our hearts and minds. Sometimes, the Spirit's direction comes immediately. Other times, it requires waiting and listening. Don't rush the process. God's timing is perfect. In prayer, be honest with your questions, but also make room for silence—allowing space for the Holy Spirit to speak.

As you pray, be attentive to recurring thoughts, deep inner peace, or a growing burden. These are often ways the Spirit reveals God's direction.

6. Follow the Peace of God

Colossians 3:15 says, "Let the peace of Christ rule in your hearts." The word "rule" here can also mean "act as an umpire." The Holy Spirit often guides through peace—or the absence of it.

If you're facing a decision and feel deep, unshakable peace, it may be a sign that the Spirit is directing you forward. Conversely, if you feel unrest or inner conflict, it may be a warning to pause or reconsider. This peace is not based on circumstances but on the Spirit's witness in your heart. Following peace doesn't mean everything will be easy, but it does mean you are walking in step with the Spirit.

7. Listen for Conviction and Correction

Part of being directed by the Holy Spirit is being open to **conviction**. John 16:8 says the Spirit will "convict the world of sin, righteousness, and judgment." This conviction isn't about shame—it's about loving correction.

When you sense the Spirit correcting your thoughts, actions, or words, respond with humility. This correction is a form of guidance—it keeps you on the path of righteousness and protects you from spiritual harm.

Ask the Spirit to search your heart daily. David prayed in Psalm 139:23-24, "Search me, God, and know my heart... See if there is any offensive way in me, and lead me in the way everlasting." Make this your prayer as well.

8. Use Discernment and Test the Spirit

Not every thought or feeling is from God. That's why it's vital to use **discernment** and test what you believe is the Spirit's leading. 1 John 4:1 warns, "Do not believe every spirit, but test the spirits to see whether they are from God." Ask yourself:
Does this align with Scripture?
Does it glorify God?
Does it promote love, humility, and truth?
Does it bear good fruit?

God's Spirit will never lead you to act in a way that contradicts His Word or character. If you're unsure, seek wise counsel from mature believers or spiritual mentors.

9. Trust God, Even When the Path Is Unclear

Being directed by the Holy Spirit doesn't always mean having a detailed roadmap. Often, God gives guidance one step at a time. Proverbs 3:5-6 encourages, "Trust in the Lord with all your heart and lean not on your own understanding; in all your ways acknowledge Him, and He will make your paths straight." Sometimes the Spirit will lead you through closed doors, delays, or detours. Trust that He sees what you can't. As you follow His lead—even when it doesn't make sense—He will reveal His purpose in time.

Conclusion

Being directed by the Holy Spirit is not reserved for a few spiritual elites—it's the privilege and responsibility of every believer. It requires a heart that is surrendered, a life grounded in Scripture, and ears open to God's voice.

As you walk closely with the Spirit, you'll begin to recognize His leading more clearly. He will guide you in truth, empower you for service, comfort you in difficulty,

and lead you into the fullness of
God's purpose for your life.
The more you trust Him, the more
you will experience the joy, peace,
and power of a Spirit-led life.

How to Receive the Holy Spirit

Receiving the Holy Spirit is one of
the most profound and
transformative experiences in a
Christian's life. The Holy Spirit is
not an abstract force or a symbolic
expression—He is the third person
of the Trinity, co-equal with God
the Father and God the Son. He is
God living within the believer,
guiding, empowering, comforting,

and transforming them into the likeness of Christ.

But what does it mean to receive the Holy Spirit? How does it happen, and what are the implications? For many, this topic is surrounded by confusion, questions, and even fear. Some associate receiving the Holy Spirit with emotional experiences or dramatic manifestations, while others see it as a quiet but powerful spiritual reality.

In this in-depth exploration, we'll examine what the Bible says about receiving the Holy Spirit, the conditions and steps involved, and what to expect afterward. Whether you're new to faith or seeking a deeper walk with God, this guide is designed to bring clarity and direction.

1. Understanding Who the Holy Spirit Is

Before we discuss how to receive the Holy Spirit, we must first understand who He is.

The Holy Spirit is the Spirit of God, sent to dwell within believers after Jesus' resurrection and ascension. Jesus promised His disciples in John 14:16-17, "And I will ask the

Father, and He will give you another Helper, that He may be with you forever; that is the Spirit of truth... He abides with you and will be in you."

The Holy Spirit is:

A Comforter (John 14:26)

A Teacher who guides us into all truth (John 16:13)

The Convicter of sin, righteousness, and judgment (John 16:8)

The Empowerer for Christian living and ministry (Acts 1:8)

The Seal of salvation (Ephesians 1:13-14)

Receiving the Holy Spirit is not about receiving a part of God; it is receiving the fullness of God's presence in a deeply personal way.

2. The Promise of the Holy Spirit

The Holy Spirit is not just for a select few or a spiritually elite group. Receiving the Holy Spirit is part of the promise of salvation.

In Acts 2, after Peter preached the gospel on the day of Pentecost, the crowd was cut to the heart and asked, "What shall we do?" Peter replied:

"Repent and be baptized, every one of you, in the name of Jesus Christ for the forgiveness of your sins. And you will receive the gift of the Holy Spirit. The promise is for you and your children and for all who are far off—for all whom the Lord our God will call." (Acts 2:38–39)

This passage makes it clear: the Holy Spirit is a gift promised to all who believe and respond to the gospel. It's not something you have to earn or qualify for by spiritual maturity. It's part of the new life in Christ.

3. The Work of the Holy Spirit at Salvation

There is sometimes confusion about whether Christians receive the Holy Spirit at the moment of salvation or later in a separate experience.

The Bible teaches that the Holy Spirit comes to dwell in the believer at the moment of true conversion. When a person puts their faith in Jesus Christ, turns from sin, and confesses Him as Lord, the Holy Spirit enters their life.

Romans 8:9 says:

"If anyone does not have the Spirit of Christ, they do not belong to Christ."

This indicates that every believer has the Holy Spirit. He regenerates (Titus 3:5), seals (Ephesians 1:13), and indwells the moment a person is saved.

However, the Bible also speaks of being filled or baptized with the Holy Spirit, which is often considered a deeper or ongoing experience of the Spirit's presence and power. We'll explore this distinction further below.

4. Steps to Receiving the Holy Spirit

A. Believe in Jesus Christ

The first and non-negotiable step to receiving the Holy Spirit is to believe in Jesus Christ as Lord and Savior.

Galatians 3:2 says:

"Did you receive the Spirit by the works of the law, or by believing what you heard?"

It is faith, not good works or religious effort, that invites the Holy Spirit into our lives. If you have not yet put your trust in Jesus, that is your starting point.

B. Repent of Sin

The Holy Spirit is holy. While He comes to us in grace, He does not dwell in hearts that cling to sin. Repentance is essential.

In Acts 2:38, Peter said, "Repent and be baptized... and you will receive the gift of the Holy Spirit." Repentance means turning from your old life and surrendering fully to God.

C. Ask in Faith

Luke 11:13 gives a beautiful promise:

"If you then, though you are evil, know how to give good gifts to your children, how much more will your Father in heaven give the Holy Spirit to those who ask him!"

Receiving the Holy Spirit is not just about doctrine—it's about desire. God responds to hearts that ask sincerely and expectantly. If you want more of the Spirit in your life, ask Him. Pray, wait, believe.

D. Surrender Completely

Receiving the Holy Spirit is not about control—it's about surrender. The Spirit fills what is empty, leads those who are willing, and empowers those who are humble.

Romans 12:1 urges believers to present themselves as "living sacrifices." If you want the Holy Spirit to fill you and guide you, you must yield your will, your desires, and your plans to God.

5. The Baptism and Filling of the Holy Spirit

Many believers experience a subsequent work of the Holy Spirit after salvation, often called the baptism or filling of the Holy Spirit. This is not about receiving more of the Spirit—as He is already present—but about the Spirit receiving more of us.

In Acts, we see several instances where believers were filled with the Holy Spirit, often resulting in boldness, spiritual gifts, and deeper intimacy with God.

Acts 2: The disciples were filled with the Spirit and spoke in other tongues.

Acts 4: They were filled again and spoke the word of God with boldness.

Acts 10: The Gentiles received the Spirit while listening to Peter preach.

Being filled with the Spirit is not a one-time event—it's a lifestyle. Ephesians 5:18 says, "Be filled with the Spirit," using a verb that implies ongoing action.

6. Signs and Evidence of Receiving the Holy Spirit

While experiences vary, Scripture outlines clear signs of the Holy Spirit's presence:

A. Inner Witness of Salvation

Romans 8:16 — "The Spirit Himself testifies with our spirit that we are God's children."

B. A New Desire for God

You begin to hunger for God's Word, prayer, and holiness.

C. Transformation of Character

Galatians 5:22-23 describes the fruit of the Spirit: love, joy, peace, patience, kindness, goodness, faithfulness, gentleness, and self-control.

D. Empowerment for Witness

Acts 1:8 — "You will receive power when the Holy Spirit comes upon you; and you will be my witnesses..."

E. Spiritual Gifts

The Holy Spirit gives gifts such as prophecy, healing, tongues, teaching, and others (1 Corinthians 12:7-11). These are for the building up of the Church and service to others.

7. Hindrances to Receiving the Holy Spirit

If someone desires the Spirit but seems unable to receive Him, certain factors may be at play:

Unrepentant sin: Clinging to sin grieves the Spirit.

Doubt or unbelief: God responds to faith.

Self-reliance: Pride blocks spiritual surrender.

Fear: Some fear losing control or being disappointed.

Wrong motives: The Spirit cannot be manipulated for personal gain.

The key is to come to God with an open heart, surrendering all and trusting Him to do His perfect work.

8. Maintaining the Presence of the Holy Spirit

Receiving the Holy Spirit is the beginning of a lifelong journey. To walk in the Spirit, you must:

Stay in the Word: The Spirit speaks through Scripture.

Pray regularly: Stay connected in conversation with God.

Obey God's voice: Follow His leading, even when it's hard.

Stay in community: The Spirit often speaks through others.

Keep your heart pure: Confess sin and guard against spiritual drift.

9. Personal Testimony and Intimacy

The ultimate goal of receiving the Holy Spirit is not power, miracles, or experiences—though those may come. The goal is intimacy with God.

The Spirit leads you into deeper love for Jesus, reveals God's heart, and transforms your life from the inside out. He teaches you to say "Abba, Father" (Romans 8:15), drawing you into the kind of relationship that defines your identity and destiny.

Conclusion

Receiving the Holy Spirit is one of the greatest gifts God offers to His children. It's not about formulas or emotions; it's about faith, surrender, and relationship. Whether you're receiving Him for the first time at salvation, or seeking a deeper filling of His presence and power, know that God longs to fill you more than you can imagine.

He is the God who gives good gifts—and the Holy Spirit is the best gift of all.

"Not by might, nor by power, but by My Spirit, says the Lord of hosts." – Zechariah 4:6

How to Discern Spirits

In a world filled with conflicting messages, spiritual voices, and supernatural claims, the ability to **discern spirits** is more important than ever. Discernment of spirits is not merely an academic or theological exercise—it is a spiritual gift and a critical survival skill in the Christian life. It enables believers to recognize what is truly from God, what is from the human soul, and what is from the enemy.

Many Christians today are confronted with situations where they must make decisions based not only on logic or facts but on spiritual realities. Whether it's determining if a message is from God, evaluating the influence behind a person's behavior, or guarding against deception in ministry or personal relationships, discerning spirits can mean the difference between truth and error, life and destruction, or growth and bondage.

So, what does it mean to discern spirits? How can one develop this discernment, and what does Scripture say about it? This in-depth guide explores the biblical foundation, practical applications,

and spiritual disciplines necessary
for discerning spirits effectively.

1. What Is the Discernment of Spirits?

The **discernment of spirits** is the
supernatural ability given by the
Holy Spirit to recognize and
distinguish between different kinds
of spiritual influence. This gift is
listed in **1 Corinthians 12:10** as
one of the manifestations of the
Spirit:

"...to another the working of
miracles, to another prophecy, to
another the ability to distinguish
between spirits..."

It allows believers to:

**Identify whether a spirit is
divine, demonic, or human**

**Recognize truth vs. deception
Judge the source of spiritual
manifestations or teachings
Protect the church and
themselves from spiritual attack
or manipulation**
Discernment is not just about
detecting evil—it's about
identifying **what is of God**. It
includes perceiving His presence,
understanding His will, and
discerning His voice from others.

2. Biblical Examples of Discerning Spirits

The Bible offers many examples of
people discerning spirits, often
with profound consequences:

A. Jesus and Peter (Matthew 16:23)

After Peter confessed Jesus as the Messiah, he rebuked Jesus for predicting His death. Jesus responded:

"Get behind me, Satan! You are a stumbling block to me."

Jesus discerned that, though Peter meant well, he was unknowingly speaking under the influence of Satan.

B. Paul and the Slave Girl (Acts 16:16–18)

A girl followed Paul's team, proclaiming, "These men are servants of the Most High God..." Her words were technically correct, but Paul discerned a demonic spirit and cast it out. This teaches us that **truthful words** can still come from a **wrong spirit**.

C. John's Admonition (1 John 4:1)

"Dear friends, do not believe every spirit, but test the spirits to see whether they are from God..."
John warns believers to **test the source** of spiritual messages and not be gullible. This discernment is crucial in a world of false prophets and spiritual deception.

3. Types of Spirits We Must Discern

To discern spirits, one must understand the **types of spiritual influences** at work:

A. The Holy Spirit

The Spirit of God always leads to truth, peace, holiness, and alignment with Scripture. His fruit includes love, joy, peace, patience, and self-control (Galatians 5:22-23).

B. Demonic Spirits

These seek to deceive, divide, destroy, and divert people from God's will. They can manifest as fear, pride, confusion, condemnation, or counterfeit miracles.

C. Human (Fleshly) Spirit

Sometimes people act or speak from their **own mind, will, or emotions**, not from any spiritual source. Discernment helps distinguish between spiritual and psychological sources.

D. Angelic Spirits

Though less common, Scripture acknowledges angels sent by God who influence and guide people

(Hebrews 1:14). Discernment helps validate their presence.

4. How to Develop Spiritual Discernment

Discernment is both a **gift** and a **discipline**. While the Holy Spirit can grant sudden insight, believers must also cultivate spiritual sensitivity over time.

A. Deepen Your Relationship with God

Discernment grows in **intimacy with God**. As you walk closely with the Lord, you become more familiar with His voice and presence.

"My sheep listen to my voice; I know them, and they follow me." (John 10:27)

Regular prayer, worship, and time in God's presence will sharpen your spiritual senses.

B. Saturate Your Mind With Scripture

God's Word is the **standard** by which all spiritual influence must be tested. The Holy Spirit will never contradict Scripture.

"For the word of God is living and active... it judges the thoughts and attitudes of the heart." (Hebrews 4:12)

The more you know the Bible, the easier it becomes to detect spiritual error or manipulation.

C. Pray for the Gift of Discernment

Ask God for the ability to discern. He promises wisdom to those who ask (James 1:5).

"To each is given the manifestation of the Spirit for the common good." (1 Corinthians 12:7)
Discernment is given not to boast, but to **protect, guide, and build up** the body of Christ.

D. Pay Attention to Inner Witnesses

The Holy Spirit often speaks through **peace, conviction, or caution**. If you sense confusion, unease, or spiritual heaviness, it may be a sign of an unclean or deceptive spirit.

Colossians 3:15 says to "let the peace of Christ rule in your hearts." No peace? Pause and pray.

E. Use Spiritual Testing Questions

When encountering a spiritual claim or experience, ask:

Does it glorify Jesus?
Is it consistent with Scripture?
Does it produce humility, love, and
righteousness?
Is it motivated by pride,
manipulation, or greed?
These tests can help you filter truth
from deception.

5. Signs of a Wrong Spirit

While some spiritual influences are
obvious, others are subtle. Here are
signs that a person or message may
be influenced by a wrong spirit:
**Twists Scripture or promotes
extra-biblical revelation**
**Draws attention to self rather
than to Jesus**
**Encourages immorality, control,
or rebellion**

Produces fear, confusion, or spiritual heaviness
Boasts supernatural power but lacks love or humility
Pushes people into emotionalism or pressure-based decisions
False prophets and counterfeit spirits can imitate truth, but they will eventually reveal themselves by their **fruit** (Matthew 7:15-20).

6. The Role of the Holy Spirit in Discernment

The Holy Spirit is the ultimate discerner of truth. Jesus called Him the "Spirit of truth" (John 16:13). He helps believers:

Interpret the Word correctly
Recognize deception or false doctrine

Discern motives in people
Avoid spiritual traps or distractions
Confirm God's will in decisions
When you are filled with the Spirit and led by Him daily, you become increasingly alert to what aligns with God and what opposes Him.

7. Common Areas Where Discernment Is Needed

A. Prophecy and Teaching

Not all who claim to speak for God are authentic. Test teachings and prophecies through Scripture and spiritual witness.

B. Relationships and Leadership

Discernment helps reveal if someone's influence in your life is godly or toxic.

C. Spiritual Movements and Practices

Many religious or supernatural practices (even within churches) are rooted in false spirits or unbiblical ideas. Stay grounded in truth.

D. Personal Thoughts and Emotions

Not every thought you have comes from God. Discernment helps you reject lies, fear, and temptation and accept truth.

8. Discerning in a World of Spiritual Confusion

We live in a time of increased spiritual deception. Media, social influencers, false teachings, and ideologies all compete for attention.

Many sound good but are **not from God**.

Paul warned in **2 Corinthians 11:14**, "Satan himself masquerades as an angel of light."

This means deception often comes dressed in sincerity, charisma, and even Scripture. Without discernment, it's easy to be led astray.

The good news? God has equipped His people with the tools to stand firm.

9. Dangers of Misusing Discernment

Like any spiritual gift, discernment must be exercised in love and humility. Misused, it can lead to:

Judgmentalism or suspicion

Spiritual pride
Witch-hunting in the church
Division or fear
True discernment is not about pointing fingers—it's about protecting truth, honoring God, and building the church.

10. Final Encouragement: Stay Anchored in Christ

Jesus is the standard of all truth. The more you know Him, the easier it is to recognize what is not of Him. Hebrews 5:14 says mature believers have "trained themselves to distinguish good from evil."
Train yourself. Stay close to Christ. Let the Holy Spirit lead you, and your spiritual sight will grow clearer every day.

Conclusion

Discerning spirits is not about being paranoid or mystical. It's about being **spiritually alert**, **biblically grounded**, and **Holy Spirit led** in a world where not everything is what it seems. It's a vital gift and practice for protecting your soul, strengthening the church, and advancing God's kingdom.

To discern spirits effectively:

Know God

Know His Word

Stay filled with the Spirit

Practice humility

Ask for wisdom

And walk in love

In doing so, you'll be equipped to navigate life with clarity, courage, and confidence—standing firm in the truth in every spiritual encounter.

Prayer to Receive the Holy Spirit
Heavenly Father, I come to You in the name of Jesus Christ, Your Son. Thank You for the gift of salvation and the promise of Your Holy Spirit. Lord Jesus, I believe that You died for my sins and rose again to give me eternal life. I repent of all my sins, and I surrender my life fully to You. Cleanse me, renew me, and make me a vessel fit for Your use. Right now, I ask You, Father, to fill me with Your Holy Spirit. I open my

heart completely and invite Your Spirit to come and dwell in me. Fill me with Your power, Your presence, and Your peace. Lead me into all truth, teach me Your ways, and guide every step I take.

I want to live for You—not by my strength, but by Your Spirit. Empower me to walk in holiness, to love like You, and to serve You faithfully. Let Your gifts flow through me for the glory of Your name. From this moment on, I yield to Your Spirit—lead me, speak to me, change me.

Thank You, Lord, for hearing my prayer. Thank You for filling me with Your Holy Spirit. I receive by faith, and I give You all the praise. In Jesus' name, **Amen.**

Thanks for reading, you can get more of this book by pasting this ASIN codes (B0F2SCSB96, B0F3DLD5N4, B0F38HDCNK) in the search bar

Made in the USA
Columbia, SC
18 June 2025

59574014R00183